
"The greatest delight of real leaders

is incubating new ones."

—Roger Fritz

"The advice in this book is priceless and timeless."

Jim Draper
Vice President
Domain Communications LLC

"This book documents the consequences when we neglect to carefully examine those we allow to be in leadership positions."

Ronald D. Stenger
Senior Vice President, CFP,
Estate Planning Specialist

"*Magnet People* is invaluable because of the sharp ways it examines *both* fakes and authentics."

Richard Sacks
President
Phoenix Co., Inc.

Other Books by Roger Fritz

Think Like a Manager

Sleep Disorders: America's Hidden Nightmare

Sales Manager's High Performance Guide: The Only Reference You Need to Build a Powerful Sales Force

A Team of Eagles

How to Manage Your Boss

The Small Business Troubleshooter

Wars of Succession

Fast Track: How to Gain and Keep Momentum

One Step Ahead, The Unused Keys to Success

Bounce Back and Win: What It Takes and How To Do It

ON CD-ROM

The Personal Business Coach, (CD-ROM)

Beyond Commitment: The Skills All Leaders Need

Magnet People

Their Secrets

and

How to Learn from Them

Roger Fritz

Meridien Marketing

Distributing Publisher:
Unlimited Publishing, LLC
Bloomington, Indiana

http://www.unlimitedpublishing.com

Contributing Publisher:
Inside Advantage Publications
1240 Iroquois Drive, Suite 406
Naperville, IL 60563
Phone: 630.420.7673
Fax: 630.420.7835
rfritz3800@aol.com

http://www.rogerfritz.com

Cover and Book Design by Charles King
Copyright © 2001 by Unlimited Publishing, LLC
This book was typeset with Adobe®. InDesign™.

Unlimited Publishing LLC provides worldwide book design, printing, marketing and distribution services for professional writers and small to mid-size presses, serving as distributing publisher. Sole responsibility for the content of each work rests with the author(s) and/or contributing publisher(s). The opinions expressed herein may not be interpreted in any way as representing those of Unlimited Publishing, nor any of its affiliates.

Copies of this book and others are available to order online at:
http://www.unlimitedpublishing.com/authors

ISBN 1-58832-033-2

Reprint Meridien Marketing
RSA 2002

Dedication

To Tom Heimsoth
•

Steadfast friend, successful entrepreneur, empathetic
employer, compassionate executive, patient listener,
practical strategist, skillful negotiator, persistent
change agent. Thanks for being a role model in my
search for magnetic leaders.

The other person deeply
involved in this project at
critical times was Anne Basye.
Her input was invaluable.

Table of Contents

Introduction

We have become much too influenced by what are usually called charismatic leaders. When I think of charismatic types, specific people come to mind. Many are politicians, of course. But some are in business, civic organizations, even religion. Most become prominent because they *seek* the limelight.

The result is, we have far too many people in leadership positions trying to be charismatic and too few who are truly magnetic. Self-centered fake leaders shrink the potential of those who follow them and perpetuate dependency.

As I started reflecting on the nature of magnetic leadership, I began to jot down lists of qualities I associated with magnetism. At first, the list contained short sentences, like these—

Charismatics tend to be selfish. Magnetics are unselfish.

Charismatics are usually takers. Magnetics are givers.

Charismatics are usually insecure and need applause. Magnetics are secure without it.

Charismatics trust words to keep loyalty. Magnetics rely on actions.

Charismatics concentrate on creating a favorable impression. Magnetics create commitment.

Charismatics focus on themselves. Magnetics focus on the cause or job to be done.

The longer I thought about it, the longer my notes grew. Sentences turned into paragraphs. Paragraphs turned into pages. Pages into chapters. The result is this book, focusing on this central question:

"What is it about a magnet person that attracts us to them, gains our respect and retains our loyalty?"

Definition:

Magnet people are exemplary mentors, leaders and character models. They attract people because they help them without expecting constant praise or unquestioning allegiance. They maintain ties because people seek their opinions, advice and companionship.

Magnet people do not necessarily have or need charisma. The basic difference is that charisma is usually turned on and off to fit circumstances. Magnet people, on the other hand, are genuine and consistent in their unselfish interactions. Their influence can be continuous; whereas once charisma declines or is lost in a particular setting, it is almost impossible to restore.

This book is about what you can do to bring out your best and become a magnet person. It is not about charisma, charm, political correctness or even social skills. Rather, it concentrates on the qualities needed by leaders to make a free society function openly and effectively without fear of tyrants, dread of bureaucrats or lure of entitlements.

Most of us say we want to live in a culture that acknowledges the importance of enduring values and practices them. Unfortunately, too many people try to take short cuts to fame, fortune and popularity by escaping the rutted lanes of hard work that lead to trust, honor, and respect. I'll bet you can list a large number of people who seemed to leapfrog to the top for mysterious reasons. I, for one, am tired of the adulation they are given—especially when so many have proven to be outright frauds.

This book aims to help you learn not only to identify magnet people, but to emulate them. The best way to ensure the proliferation of legitimate leaders and magnet people is to become one yourself! The more worthy people, the less room there is for self-centered counterfeits.

Start anywhere. Turn to any page. We want to open your eyes and mind to who is worthy of being followed, why, and how to learn from them.

Roger Fritz

Chapter 1

Magnet People Are Genuine

Magnet people are genuine. They know who they are, so they don't need to pretend to be somebody—anybody!—else. They don't need to deceive. Their self-knowledge frees them to focus on what they want to do...and get it done.

People who know themselves can count on themselves. And if they can trust themselves, you can trust them too. That's why the second element of being genuine is being trustworthy. Just think of the definitions of the words *truth* and *lie*. "Genuine" is practically a synonym for true. False, on the other hand...well, you get the picture.

Genuine people keep things simple. They don't need to spin confusing tales. They don't need to impress or fool anyone. On the contrary—their ideas speak for themselves.

They aren't impressed by hot air, either. Genuine people can spot an impostor a mile away. Flashiness never fools them. In friends, colleagues, and employees, they prize accountability over credentials. All the degrees in the world matter less than the ability to keep your word.

Genuine people lead by example—"do as I do," not "do what I say." Their daily lives become templates of unselfish, caring and exemplary behavior.

Genuine People Have the Greatest Impact on Their Organization

An organization's culture reflects the most deeply held values and behaviors of a handful of individuals—the CEO and senior executives. In a small, privately held company, the culture is influenced by a single individual—usually the founder/owner.

The more genuine, trustworthy and accountable this individual, the more these values will permeate the organization. A culture of personal leadership and solid values gives a company a strong competitive advantage in a business environment. They don't have to constantly look over their shoulders to see if they have been caught in a lie. Their suppliers know they will be paid on time. Their employees know the company will meet payroll and follow through on promised benefits.

Know yourself better than anybody

Be sure you are trustworthy

Keep it simple

Prize accountability over credentials

Know Yourself Better Than Anybody

The recipe for success can be expressed in three words: **know yourself first**.

When you know who you are, what you value most, and what you can do best, you can match your gifts to a career and find work that best fits it.

Magnet people enjoy what they do and do it well. They avoid the torture of the wrong career endured just for money or prestige. They frequently are leaders—because true leadership is authentic self-expression. It is the ultimate indication of empowerment. People wrapped up in the wrong job—in trying to fool others about their skills, sincerity, or commitment—aren't expressing themselves authentically because they are too focused on discontent. **The best leaders nurture and release the best that is in their followers.**

Have you ever noticed what happens when you are around people who are insincere or artificial? You feel edgy, uncomfortable. In contrast, magnet people are easy to be with. They radiate confidence that puts people at ease.

That's because they know they can count on themselves. Their sense of self-reliance, their keen trust in their own abilities frees them to trust and like others—and frees others to trust and like them. After all, if you don't believe in yourself, why should anyone believe in you?

Admiral Robert E. Peary's belief in himself and his goals sustained him through the eight trips and 23 years it took for him to accomplish his life's ambition: reaching the North Pole. "I shall find a way or make one," he declared. His self-reliance and determination was also praised by Norwegian explorer Fridtjof Nansen: "I do not know what I admire most with Peary—the indefatigable energy with which he works year after year...or the never-failing readiness with which he overcomes the greatest and most unexpected difficulties."

Take charge of your life. Dream at night.
In daylight, act.

Do You Really Know Yourself?

What prompts your actions?

Do they flow from deep within you? Or are they motivated by something more superficial—perhaps an external personality that you have adopted, or your notion of what others expect?

Magnet people act from their basic character—from who they are inside and out. Their actions express their real personality. That doesn't mean their inner self is always on display. While we often need to protect our innermost feelings, I have observed that magnet people tend to respond to challenges from their deepest impulses and beliefs. Important decisions and actions require authenticity. You don't need to tap into your deepest character to decide which shoes to wear in the morning, or to respond to a routine memo. But when the stakes are highest, your character will count most.

How can you identify your gifts of authenticity and self-awareness?

The first way is to seek responsibility, as early as possible and as often as possible. Accepting new challenges and responsibilities helps you identify areas of strength that set you apart (and maybe some areas you're better off passing to others). As you become more and more able to pinpoint and polish areas of special expertise, you gain a distinct competitive advantage. Avoiding responsibility, on the other hand, is a sure-fire way to let your gifts lay fallow while others pass you by.

Another key to discovering your strengths and abilities is to cultivate originality and independence. "Blaze your own way, make your own path, or you will never make many impressions in the world," says Ken Shelton, publisher of *Personal Excellence* magazine. He believes that originality will always attract attention and admiration—because we will always admire people who have the courage to lift their heads, who dare to step to the front and declare themselves.

To cultivate independence, take charge of your life. Don't jump into new roles without thinking. Whatever you are now, you can be better. Your future is not written in stone. It's a changing horizon.

Finally, set aside time for reflection. Magnet people have given a lot of thought to who they are. Through reflection, meditation, writing, solitude, and worship, they have come to know themselves and their strengths. They are not afraid to act, but they think first. Follow their lead and take time to contemplate. In a busy life, an hour of thinking can be critical. Invest in yourself. Turn off the TV. Spend an hour every day focusing on what is important to you, and why you are doing what you are doing. Write down your answers.

Be honest about your talents, your gifts, your desires, your feelings, and your values. As you do this, the real you will prevail in more and more situations and you will be judged more accurately for who you are and what you can do. And when you are genuine—"your own author" says leadership expert Warren Bennis—your authenticity and trustworthiness will show.

What Are Your Values?

You can't be genuine at the core unless you know your values. When you know what you value, you can tell right away when you're asked to go against them. You know when decisions you make feel good, because they enforce your values. Values give you a framework for setting goals and making choices.

Start with these questions.

What do I value most in life?

What do I live for?

What would I be willing to die for?

What do I prize most? If my life were threatened by illness or danger, what would I miss most? What would I defend first?

A long list is not required. Five or six will let you derive goals and habits that will sustain you because they are compatible with the values at your core.

What lies behind or ahead of us is less important than what lies within.

Understand Your Own Value

Magnet people have a keen sense of their own worth. From it they derive a sense of the worth of those around them. Magnet people especially understand that every human being is uniquely significant—and that each person's gifts can make a difference.

When you understand the significance of your own gifts, you can begin to envision how to best use them. Magnet people feel a sense of duty to use their gifts and talents unselfishly, beyond their own benefit. That's the difference between self-esteem and self-importance. **Self-esteem drives us to use our special gifts for others. Self-important people believe the world revolves around them.** People with solid characters value themselves, but they see beyond themselves in valuing what others need and can do.

Magnet people also regularly assess their gifts and strive to sharpen them. Naturalist Edward O. Wilson, a leading scientist, educator, and author of *Sociobiology* and *On Human Nature*, has assessed his strengths and weaknesses ruthlessly. "Probe in all directions and learn where your abilities are exceptional, where mediocre, where poor," he recommends. "Then fashion tactics to achieve the best possible results. And never give up hope." Throughout his remarkable career, he has worked to offset his weaknesses by teaming with colleagues with complementary talents.

You can do the same. Speaker Denis Waitley uses a simple exercise to help people assess their strengths and weaknesses. Make a list with two columns. On one side, write "I am good at..." and on the other, "I need improvement in." Pick your ten best traits and your ten limiting traits. Take a moment to appreciate your assets, and then take the first three traits you don't like about yourself and plan how you'll change them. Or, like Edward O. Wilson, seek others whose strengths can make up for your weaknesses.

While it's important to strive for self-improvement, it's critical to practice self-acceptance. When you accept yourself, you become realistic about who you are, what you believe, your strengths and your limitations. When you believe in your own potential, you can make more accurate plans and goals for fulfilling that potential. Your honesty about your own gifts and shortcomings will help you to be more honest with others. In a way, self-acceptance is your moment of truth. As Mark Twain said, "A man cannot be comfortable without his own approval." Accept yourself for what you are—and then strive to your very limits.

Believe that life is worth living, and your belief will create the fact.

—William James, psychologist and philosopher

Be Trustworthy

Trust is the glue that binds all relationships and agreements, personal and corporate. Trust begets trust. Because magnet people trust themselves, they can readily trust others who deserve it. Their deep self-knowledge yields self-trust and is the font of true leadership. Their ability to act in ways that express their basic nature and deepest values enables them to avoid the pitfalls that plague pretenders. They develop a personal yardstick for measuring themselves and their gifts.

They can confidently express their own ideas and see them through.

For baseball executive Bill Veeck, owner of three major league and two minor league baseball teams, trust in his own abilities and dreams translated into trust in others. Confident about his own dreams, he was confident enough to listen to what fans had to say, whether they called him at home or met him at the stadium during a game. Because he believed in doing the right thing, he helped integrate baseball by hiring the second black major league player, who later became the second black team manager.

To improve your self-trust,

1. View yourself as unique. Don't try to fit into other people's molds.
2. Listen to the "inner voice" that defines what is right.
3. Seek responsibility and welcome it. It is your growth hormone.
4. Don't stay in a rut waiting for someone to dig you out.

Self-trust gives you several distinct advantages. It enables you to recognize and rely on your abilities. It gives you confidence to cope with more difficult situations than you have faced before. And it provides you with the decisiveness to push for results that may lack popular support.

"There's a Whole Lotta Cheatin' Going On!"

Two kinds of cheating can break trust: cheating others, and cheating yourself.

Broken trust is not easy to repair. Breaking promises, lying, compromising people and cheating break the bonds that tie people together. "I'm sorry" isn't enough to restore trust to a former level.

When we cheat ourselves, we are not usually aware of it. But we cheat ourselves when we...

- settle for less than our best
- refuse a difficult assignment
- overlook or don't report a crime
- allow politicians to mortgage our future
- accept something for nothing.

Be honest with yourself first, and then tell others the truth. Because trust and integrity *do* matter. **Integrity does not break, it crumbles.** People remain loyal to those who treat them fairly, and who act with integrity.

Everyone knows the story of Mohandas Gandhi, whose incredible personal integrity helped lead his country to independence from Great Britain. But many lesser-known people count on integrity to lead and to inspire loyalty.

Integrity makes Saturn president Cynthia Trudell, the first woman to head a major U.S. car company, stand out in her industry. Her willingness to keep her word has helped heal the rift between labor and management and encouraged a new labor-management partnership that rewards productivity and gives workers a say in how the company is run.

Remove integrity, and what is left is a shadow. A survey of 2,300 employees conducted by the Hudson Institute and Walker Information revealed that more than half thought their company leaders lacked integrity. Only 42 percent believed their organizations deserved their loyalty, and only one in four employees considered him or herself "truly loyal." To the interviewees, integrity was an important ingredient in deciding whether to stay or go. When a lack of integrity triggers compromised ethics, people are more likely to leave the job. And when employees go, so do customers. The average American company loses half of its employees every four years—and half of its customers every five years!

What other evidence is needed to prove that integrity—or the lack thereof—has a significant impact on everything from the top of an organization to the very bottom line?

Character is what you are, and reputation is what people think you are. But if your reputation is bad, you might as well have a bad character.

—Pete Rozelle

Winning the Character Battles

People who are genuine have character. They are known for their self-discipline, compassion, and courage. They have molded their character in the crucible of daily successes and failures.

They know that actions can become habits, and accumulated habits form character—that a habit of lying quickly erodes character. And that a habit of cheating, fudging details, taking more credit than deserved or misrepresenting the facts leads to becoming untrustworthy.

Proof is in the headlines every day. In Illinois, newspapers uncovered evidence of bribery in the former Secretary of State's office, which issues drivers' licenses. For as little as $20, test personnel were willing to pass and issue licenses to people who didn't even know how to start a car, or to commercial truck drivers who had never sat behind the wheel of a semi. The lives and families destroyed by the malfeasance of these unprepared drivers—and these government employees who traded their integrity for a few dollars—has only increased suspicion about the competence and integrity of so-called "public servants." Too many highly-placed politicians have had dishonest careers starting with little incidents.

Character is formed not by what happens to you but by what you do about what happens. It does not develop in tranquility, but in trial, error and resilience. Chapter 2, on Diligence, is filled with anecdotes about people who have had to overcome real obstacles and recover from life-threatening setbacks. Their stories are featured because they used these trials to build their character—not run from adversity.

The price you pay for lack of character is facing a world where you are not trusted.

Loyalty is the earned outcome of trust. When trust is earned and deserved, loyalty will follow.

Magnet people who succeed in gaining trust teach with their lives more than their words. They lead by example. They know that people respect leaders who know what it's like in the trenches. In their organizations, they seek to develop relationships of trust by modeling behavior that can be trusted. They do what they say, speak truthfully, and refuse to act from petty self-interest.

Marvin Bower, a founder of the consulting firm McKinsey and Company, spoke courageously and truthfully. He once told the head of a company that *he* was his company's problem. When he instructed his people to accept only work that was necessary and that McKinsey could do well, he set the example by turning down work from Howard Hughes and a government contract to develop a bail-out plan for American Motors. He never worried about turning down business. "If we do the right work for the client, we'll make more money," he said:.

Genius is admired

Wealth is envied

Power is feared

Character is trusted

Keep It Simple

There are a couple of ways to define this phrase.

First, "keep it simple" means "no smoke and mirrors."

The best leaders always keep things simple. As General Colin Powell tells companies, the visions of effective leaders "are lean and compelling, not cluttered and buzz-word laden. Their decisions are crisp and clear, not tentative and ambiguous." To Powell's mind, simplicity creates clarity of purpose, leadership, and integrity.

His experience has also led him to be somewhat suspicious of experts. "Don't be buffaloed by experts," he says. "Policies that emanate from ivory towers often have an adverse impact on the people out in the field who are fighting the wars or bringing in the revenues." I wholeheartedly agree. Those who try to impress with complicated solutions often want to see others fail!

Marvin Bower of McKinsey knew how to cut through a complicated problem to find its simple roots. Knowing that a strong organization depends on strong basics, he kept his consultants focused on the basics no matter how distracting and complex the problem. Instead of starting with the solution, his firm worked to find the problem first. Instead of approaching a client with a theory, he had his consultants get to the root of the problem by talking to everyone from the executive suite to the janitor's closet.

Fritz Shurmur, defensive coach for the Green Bay Packers, the St. Louis Rams, and the Seattle Seahawks, also stuck to the basics. "The coach has to break down each technique into steps or phases," he said. He would teach the simplest phase of a technique first, and then move to steps of increasing difficulty. By breaking the game of football into simple steps, he taught countless defensive players his methods and helped the Green Bay Packers win the Super Bowl.

Magnet people also know how to use simple language to cut through argument, debate and doubt to offer a solution everybody can understand. Simple language was a key to Mohandas Gandhi's success. To reach the poor and uneducated, he used simple language and powerful Hindu religious symbols to communicate his message of nonviolent resistance. He also used positive language. Instead of criticizing the British, he spoke about the greatness of the cause of independence.

Keeping it simple also means focusing on what is most important. Queen Elizabeth I is a good example. Committed to being the best queen she could, upon her coronation she declared herself "married to England." She kept her eye on the biggest goals, and England thrived, thanks to her simple, dogged, single-minded focus on her country's good.

Explorer Roald Amundsen also practiced this kind of single-mindedness. "My career has been a steady progress toward a definite goal since I was 15 years of age," he wrote. Determined to become an explorer, he worked to get himself physically fit, honed his seafaring skills so he could lead expeditions as both sea captain and explorer, and talked to as many explorers as he could to absorb their knowledge. To reach his goal of sailing the Northwest Passage between the Atlantic and Pacific oceans and, later, of reaching the South Pole, he learned tent design, ice cutting, and how to lead teams of dogs. His focus paid off; both his goals were realized.

"Keeping it simple" runs against the grain of our cluttered and distracted society. But slowing down long enough to discover one's focus can be difficult. Says author and simplicity guru Elaine St. James, "Maintaining a complicated life is a great way to avoid changing it...there's nothing more 'dangerous' than having a little time on your hands."

Don't be afraid of a little free time. It's absolutely essential to achieving self-knowledge and self-trust. If you don't know what you're doing, or you are at sea in a needlessly complicated and meaningless existence, stop. Rethink what you are doing. Do what it takes to set your real goals, and then ruthlessly eliminate unnecessary activities or responsibilities that may be distracting you.

But don't set too many goals. One or two will be plenty. Roald Amundsen set two life goals and achieved them both. To do so, he capitalized on his strengths and found others who could complement his weaknesses. He didn't dissipate his efforts by trying to do everything.

Simplify and concentrate. Do something that makes you different, that gives you a clear competitive advantage. Don't try to be all things to all people. Maintain your general skills but develop one or two areas where you can perform brilliantly.

Simplicity is a matter of focus. When you know what is important to you, you can organize your life around it. Your concentration will have the power of a laser beam, and you will achieve your goals.

Whether it's direct language or a short list of goals, simplicity is almost always well received. In an era when composition students were urged to write music that was complex and dissonant, classical composer Darius Milhaud encouraged one of his students to go against the grain. "Never be afraid of something that people can whistle or remember," he told Burt Bacharach. Following his teacher's advice led Bacharach to compose dozens of memorable tunes that earned him a place in the Songwriters Hall of Fame.

In short: simplify, don't complicate. And beware of those who do!

You are not successful until someone brags that they sat beside you in grade school.

Prize Accountability Over Credentials

Magnet people are accountable. They are willing to accept responsibility for getting something done.

Seth Godin, author of *Permission Marketing,* calls these kinds of people Torchbearers and defines them as people who "stand up, look everyone in the eye and say, I'll make it happen!"According to Godin, torchbearers:

- don't make excuses.
- often attract a crowd, because people are fascinated by folks who are willing to carry responsibility. Some are willing to follow the torchbearer uphill as well as downhill.
- don't realize how unique they are, how powerful their role is, or how hard their task is—but they do it anyway.

- care more about forward motion than they do about which route to take. They don't look for perfect solutions. "They keep moving, because they realize that moving is the best way to get where they're going."
- don't stop until they finish.

In a sense, magnet people are torchbearers because they lead and teach by example. While they may not use inspirational words, their actions inspire. Followers are welcome but not absolutely necessary to feed their ego or stimulate them to greater accomplishment.

They certainly don't pass the flame. "People who are busy pointing fingers and whining about "those guys" are demonstrating they're not torchbearers," Godin points out.

Another element of accountability is moral courage. Larry Smith of Harvard's Kennedy School of Government says that often ideas are not enacted for lack of moral courage. "General Grant used to say that he knew officers who would risk their lives in battle, but who lacked 'the moral courage' to make decisions for which they would be held accountable," he points out. Too often, he says, people want someone else to make the decision, or they will sit on a new idea until someone else approves it and makes their actions safe.

"Any clever person can make plans for winning a war if he has no responsibility for carrying them out," said Winston Churchill about those who criticized his strategies for preparing the British navy for World War I. His branch of the military was the only one ready when war suddenly broke out in July 1914.

Accountability can be lonely—even in today's informal, collaborative corporate culture. When the buck stops with you, it's up to you to make tough choices that impact the fate of those around you. No wonder those Civil War generals preferred one-to-one combat to leading the charge.

Who Will Do What by When?

The key to accountability is determining **who** will do **what** by **when**. James Papada III, CEO of Technitrol Inc., knows this well.

He doesn't just give responsibility and require accountability. He breaks responsibilities into action items for specific "owners." Every objective is broken into tiny, accountable pieces. Then he assigns return dates and follow-up meetings for each item. Missing dates is serious business, but meeting objectives and accomplishing action items is rewarded by significant bonuses.

Papada uses delegation and relentless follow-up to turn his vision into reality. To him, details matter. Constant communication facilitates the process. He talks to every manager once a day in the corporate headquarters and meets with offsite managers via telephone weekly.

Accountability—The Only Road to Success

You won't become a magnet person until you are accountable. And it will be difficult to achieve anything at all if you are surrounded by people who are *not* accountable. Select ONLY accountable people. Never knowingly put anybody on your payroll who will always be dependent on you to tell them what to do. Don't create dependency and don't perpetuate it. Have you ever said to yourself about your children, "My job from the day these people came into this world is to keep them dependent on me?" Of course not!

To me, accountable people are bullet-biters. In the old western movies, a bullet-biter was someone who had an arrow dug out with a hunting knife, as he bit on a bullet and bore the pain. They are tough people. They know how to handle problems, even extreme adversity. To find accountable people, you have to look for a stack of bitten bullets.

I've bitten a few myself. When I was 15 years old I had polio. My left leg is two and a half inches longer, two and a half inches less in circumference. But I think polio was one of the best things that ever happened to me. Sound weird? Well, first, I'm alive. A lot of people had polio and died. Also, at that tender age I realized that after I did every exercise the doctors prescribed, prayed every prayer I knew, my dangling leg was not going to be normal. So I decided that if I couldn't compete in the same athletic arenas as before, I would compete with my mind to show people I was not totally handicapped. Especially, I vowed to show that I was not a mental cripple.

Magnet people have sought out challenges, overcome adversity, and worked to stretch themselves. They also challenge others to think so that they will gain the confidence they need to accomplish ever more difficult tasks. I call this the confidence circle.

Confidence grows with achievement. More confidence nurtures more achievement. You wouldn't build confidence by appointing a son or a daughter to a job for which they are not qualified. Such an action might in fact shatter confidence—theirs and those around them. Don't bring in people who fool you with their credentials or their good intentions. You don't build strong organizations with those kinds of people. All you do is nurture their confidence in their deception.

Defining performance expectations builds confidence. (For more on performance, see Chapter 3, "Magnet People Are Objective.") You want your expectations to be as clear as possible so people know how they will be evaluated. Follow James Papada's lead and break responsibilities down into small bites—and once expectations are clear, follow up on performance regularly!

This exercise will help accountable people grow. Certain people—the ones who end up being magnet people—grow up seeking responsibility. They seem to live by the motto, "Send me." They also seek out those who will accept responsibility, and surround themselves with the best. They look for intelligent, curious people with high ethical standards, strong ambition, and drive. These people welcome clear expectations and high performance standards.

I've found it's better to be involved with good people in a bad situation than bad people in a good situation. Empowered people who are not accountable spin their wheels and waste your time. In any organization, no matter what your role, seek accountability. And quickly weed out those who avoid it!

We are what we repeatedly do.

Excellence, therefore,

is not an act

but a habit.

—Aristotle

Accountability in the Non-profit Sector

I'm pleased to see increasing evidence that accountability is recognized as an important factor. Many people are no longer bamboozled by credentials.

These days, accountability is even penetrating the nonprofit sector, as new "venture philanthropists" with Silicon Valley and dot-com fortunes look for ways they can improve the world. Before they hand over sizeable sums to their favorite charities, these new philanthropists want evidence of good planning. They want to see how much of each dollar goes to overhead and how much gets to the intended beneficiaries. Some ask for multi-year business plans and projections that show how needs will be met. They ask for plans for growth, and want to see evidence that a charity is meeting benchmarks. In short, they want accountability. And when accountability leads to evidence that their contributions are making a difference, they give even more generously.

―――――――――――――――――

Usually if you're willing to be in charge,

someone will put you there.

―――――――――――――――――

Chapter 2

Magnet People Are Diligent

Diligence is the mother of good luck.

Some Things Simply Never Go Out of Style...

...like diligence, persistence, and plain old hard work. Expressions like *"the early bird gets the worm"* are still part of our everyday language because there's *still* nothing like hard work when it comes to preparing to succeed.

Computers, e-mail, fax machines, and cell phones have shaved off time and boosted our productivity, but they aren't a short cut around all hard work.

That's even true in Silicon Valley, where workplaces boast private chefs, lap pools, exercise equipment, and bunk beds. Those amenities are offered because people who commit to those companies often work around the clock.

Persistence, diligence, and inclination to "get at it" are hallmarks of magnet people—yesterday, today, and tomorrow.

Because magnet people are diligent, they can lead by example, and encourage others to do as they *do*—not just as they say.

But diligence is more than working hard.

It means persisting—especially when things look tough. Before he made it big, country music star Willie Nelson spent years playing behind a chicken wire fence in obscure honky-tonks. Why the fence? To protect musicians from rowdy customers.

Those days are a memory now, but Nelson says that every successful person he has known has spent a lot of time "behind the chicken wire."

That's true for Deloris Jordan. Before she became known as the mother of the most famous basketball player in the world, she parented five children in obscurity. It was hard work, and it demanded a consistent measure of discipline and love. She and her late husband, James, put in thousands of hours with Michael and his siblings. She was always involved. She and James went to every one of their children's games. They went to church together. Took their kids on vacations. And when one parent said no, so did the other. They worked as a team, supporting each other in the most difficult but rewarding job they knew.

Diligence—showing up, staying committed, and working hard—took Michael Jordan and his parents to the top. Even now Deloris Jordan works hard. At last count she had raised more than $7 million for charities and foundations. Hardly retirement!

An essential ingredient in Deloris Jordan's personal development is her strong sense of personal responsibility. She was willing to work hard and devote an above-average amount of time and energy in pursuit of her goals. In my view, that is diligence.

Through diligence, people grow and get better over time. Not because they keep doing things faster and faster, but because they think all the time about what they are doing and why. There is a difference between efficiency and effectiveness. Efficiency is doing things right. **Effectiveness is doing the *right* things *right*.** What difference does it make if you're busily engaged doing the wrong things?

You can get farther on guts than on instinct. By guts, I mean persistence. Many people who aren't very bright make it because they just don't know how or when to quit. **Remember, brain power without willpower is no power.** And willpower can take you a long way!

Diligence also has a lot to do with not giving in to immediate gratification. Those who crave immediate satisfaction never learn to plan to make their future better than their past. Giving in now leads to defeat later. By disciplining ourselves and our appetites, we master enduring values...acquire lasting skills...and achieve the adaptation and flexibility to thrive in good times and bad.

Magnet people are their own power source.

Magnet people don't dwell long on their successes.

Magnet people make themselves needed.

Magnet people get up one more time— and try again.

Be Your Own Power Source

Magnet people don't look outside themselves for power. They dislike coattails and are suspicious of unearned credentials. Instead, they are curious...work hard to discover their own strengths...seek knowledge...burnish their skills to a high polish...and strive to meet their own high standards of personal excellence. Their personal power flows from these ingredients.

Superficial diplomas and awards are irrelevant to the development of personal power. I've never met anyone of substance who derived **lasting** power from someone else. The best ideas I've seen come from people who believe in them—not from those who are only repeating what the highest-ranking people say.

Recently, some of the most powerful people around are entrepreneurs. They derive power and satisfaction from the process of building a company from the ground up. Probably the best example is Bill Gates. No federal subsidies, grants, or trust funds made Microsoft successful. Instead, bright people with great ideas worked in teams, lived within frugal budgets, and followed simple lines of authority. Even today, its 31,000 employees work in a non-hierarchical atmosphere. Offices are all the same size and support-staff are few. Passionate people seeking new challenges can build their own power based on their good ideas. And Bill—well, his main challenge is still finding ways to incubate new ideas.

Entrepreneurs especially find that how they use their personal power establishes the culture of their companies. When power leads to action, even the smallest acts of a leader make a difference. The moods of the person in charge affect everyone...how they talk to people, whether or not they take the time to get to know them, how they handle customers and clients. The example set by the leader permeates the organization. Knowing this, it's a good idea to keep in mind the words of William James, the father of modern psychology, who summed up personal power when he said, "I will act as if what I do makes a difference."

Developing your own power source takes faith. Robert Johnson, founder of the Black Entertainment Network and the wealthiest African American, says, "Ask any entrepreneur about his rock, and he'll tell you he has a mountain. You have to have faith in what you're doing, and go after something with the conviction that there's nothing more important than making it happen." He knows because magnet people's faith fuels an attitude that is powerful and optimistic. They focus on what works, not on what doesn't. And while they engage life with optimism, they maintain a sense of gratitude and few regrets.

The magnet pathway is less open to those who derive their power from others—because they are always afraid of making a mistake and alienating the source of their power. Power derived or inherited from others can be perilously short-term. It must be exercised daily, and it requires constant alertness. This slavish need to guard short-term power is kept alive by the loser's lament, "I was only doing what I was told." People who are their own power source are freer to do the right thing. Unhampered by fears about what someone else might think or expect, they can stand up for what is right and act on their own values, not compromise them!

Power Can Incubate New Competencies

Power can stimulate and influence many more people to develop their talents. Craig Binette is Vice President and General Manager of Polyester Resins at DuPont. He's been trying for a long time to determine whether beer drinkers would accept plastic beer bottles. Instead of using focus groups or outside consultants, he turned the problem over to a group of insiders. The DuPont Leadership for Growth program uses the company's top 400 executives to form teams to solve problems involving over 200 product groups. For three weeks, teams concentrate on fresh ideas and strategize to gain new revenues. No team member is assigned a project in his or her division. Each brings different background and skills. Together, teams get the tools, travel budgets, and data they need. It works! Participants enjoy the contrast to normal work routines and the stimulation and challenge of finding new revenue streams. Oh yes, the plastic beer bottles...The team discovered that, because beer sales are flat in the U.S, brewers are anxious to be distinctive. So the next step is to partner with a brewer selling beer in plastic bottles at sports stadiums with their own logo.

There is a close relationship between power and responsibility. You only retain your power when you take responsibility for your actions. And when you do, you can discover the source of power in a five-letter word: SERVE. **The smallest supportive action is better than the grandest intention.** The greatest rewards begin when you change from "What's in it for me?" to "How can I help you?"

_____

Words to Live By

The four most challenging words,

"Get up, move on."

The four most inspirational words,

"I believe you can."

The four most soothing/comforting words,

"We'll work it out."

The four most destructive words,

"I know you can't."

The four most compassionate words,

"I'll take your place."

The four most instructional words,

"Let me show you."

_____

Don't Dwell on Your Successes

You'd think Mike Shanahan would take a breather after his Denver Broncos won the Super Bowl.

Instead of dwelling on his success, he and his team got right back to work to make sure they'd win again—and they did, the very next year.

Most people think successes are meant to be savored indefinitely. But one success doesn't make a lifetime, and Mike Shanahan knows it.

So does former presidential candidate and basketball star Bill Bradley. To him, victory is a more subtle threat than defeat. "Sustaining focus after a failure isn't a problem—indeed, it might even sharpen your alertness, because you're intent on making up for your mistake," he says. "It's after you've pulled off a great play that focus is difficult, because there is a strong temptation to dwell on what you just did. By the time you finish congratulating yourself, the opponent has scored three baskets."

Natural ability has a lot to do with success in athletics, but diligence plays an even bigger role. People who achieve the highest level of success have an unbelievable work ethic, and they aren't afraid to make sacrifices.

Wide receiver Jerry Rice is a good example. Already one of the greatest players of all time, his strategy before the Super Bowl games was to watch opponents closely. He would determine which players were best, and devote time to observing their methods and studying their behavior. Instead of dwelling on his own successes, he proudly acknowledged them, and worked harder to be even better.

"The time to prepare for your next expedition is when you have just returned from a successful trip."

—Admiral Robert E. Peary
First to reach the North Pole

If it's important not to dwell on your successes, it's even more important not to dwell on your failures.

The secret to success in business—and in life—is determined largely by how we deal with failure. Some failure is certain, for no one can win all the time. In fact, a diet of constant victory would be bad indeed. It would discourage us from taking new risks. The challenge is to prepare for success while adjusting to and learning from the inevitable setbacks.

Here are eight guidelines that will serve you well.

1. Accept the fact that you are not perfect, nor is anyone else. We all make mistakes. The surest way to avoid failure is to do nothing, but then you will get nowhere. Give yourself permission to fail once in awhile. Avoiding failure is not the same as success.
2. Determine whether it is failure that disturbs you or the rejection that's often associated with it. If it is fear of being branded a loser, regain your confidence quickly by doing something well, then fear of failure will no longer haunt you.
3. Decide which is more important: avoiding failure, or doing something worthwhile. If you're constantly

striving to do something worthwhile, you'll have no time
to worry about an occasional failure. In other words,
believe in your product or service.

4. Don't be intimidated by failure. Realize that failure
is one of the Laws of Life. Learn to be somewhat
fatalistic about it. Everyone who has ever bought a
lottery ticket knows that there's very little likelihood of
success. Everyone who has ever played a card game—or
a board game like Monopoly—knows that there must be
a loser as well as a winner; and although we all play to
win, the odds usually are at least 50-50 that we will lose.
So it is in life. You win some and you lose some. The
secret is to try to win more often than you lose, and try
never to lose in critical situations.

5. Separate personal failures from team failures. If the
quarterback on a football team gets sacked, he's not a
failure. He failed to get the play away because someone
else failed to provide a block. The blocker isn't totally to
blame, either. Nine out of ten times, he does his job well.
A single miscue does not make him a failure. Remember:
his opponent was trying just as hard to be successful
as he was.

The key to recovery from failure is...

Let it go so you can grow.

The key to dealing with success...

Let it go so you can grow.

---

6. Don't use blame as a means of making failure more personally tolerable. You can't really kid yourself. All you can do is add a layer of guilt to your discomfort. Analyze the failure to see WHAT caused it, not WHO. Then take steps to see that this situation will not occur again.
7. Accept failure as a part of the learning process. As children, we learn to walk by standing, falling, rising, trying, falling, and trying again. Eventually, we master the process. Along the way, we learn a little more from every failure.
8. Don't dwell on failures. A single defeat is not a final defeat. In fact, temporary defeat is the mother of greatness. Maintaining a confident, positive attitude about yourself and what you are doing is critical, not only to your future performance, but to your personal happiness.

Move on. Don't let your failures keep defeating you and don't dwell long on your successes. Go on to new ones. People who dwell too long on successes are living in the past. Over the years I have found that people who keep talking about the past are missing the present and resisting the future—not a good recipe for success. Magnet people uphold lasting values, but they don't impede the rush of change. They try to anticipate it and use it to their advantage.

Twenty-eight-year-old Lance Armstrong, many believe, is the greatest bicycle racer in the world after winning the 1999 and 2000 2,300 mile three-week Tour de France. Yet only three years earlier he was fighting for his life. Testicular cancer had spread to his lungs and brain. As he battled to recover he took a long-term view and adopted as his motto, "Make every negative a positive." It's what kept him going. "In a bike race you don't fly up a hill," he says. "You struggle slowly and painfully. Then, maybe, if you work hard enough, you get to the top ahead of everybody else." His fame is living testimony not just to racing skills, but more importantly, to the power of resilience.

I have more important things to do than to spend my time in worrying over what happened yesterday. My time today is taken up preparing for tomorrow. I have more important things to do than pitying myself.

—Franklin A. Seiberling
Founder of Goodyear Tire & Rubber

It seems every time you turn around, another Silicon Valley start-up has gone down the tubes—and with it, its lavishly compensated CEO. In most business cultures, failure—especially the bankruptcy of one's company—is cause for humiliation. The rules are different in Silicon Valley. Top management seems to recover and move on quickly to new opportunities. And failure is almost a credential.

Jim Cathcart, author of *The Acorn Principle*, advises people to lighten up to reduce stress. "When life isn't fair to you, get over it quickly. Take your misfortunes as "course corrections" rather than "catastrophes," he says. "Let go so you can grow." In the face of success or failure, growth is resilience.

Most failures don't realize how close they
were to success when they gave up.

Failure is—

a learning experience

a necessary pathway to success

an opportunity to try something new.

Make Yourself Needed

In my view, the secret to success in our world is to make yourself needed.

When others need you, you will be acknowledged. Consulted. Respected. And compensated fairly, or better. You're also unlikely to be neglected, downsized, or fired—unless the people at the top of your organization are insane!

How exactly can you make yourself needed?

- See what needs to be done before others do
- Spot problems before they become serious and volunteer to fix them
- Don't burn your bridges...make and keep allies
- Become expert in areas others avoid.

Making yourself needed is the direct opposite of relying on credentials. Credentials can be very shallow. They may get you into the ballpark, but they won't help you play the game. Players must have the ability to get results.

To me, results are the foundation on which magnet people view the world. They keep results in mind as they select people for projects and key positions.

People who are results-oriented are hard to fool. They aren't dazzled by subterfuge. With results as their criterion, they can distinguish between substance and smoke.

In a world cluttered with hype, we need an even greater emphasis on performance and results. Far too many people with no experiential base have gained undeserved acclaim. Politicians are notorious for their eagerness to claim credit for the hard work of average tax-paying citizens.

People who are needed are referenceable. When you are reference-able, it's easy for others to confirm your accomplishments and your track record with anyone you refer to them.

Remember: the more you need your boss, the less your boss needs you. **Do yourself a favor and devote yourself to being needed, not needing.**

Andrew Carnegie certainly did. Although he had only five years of schooling, he tried to learn all he could about the jobs he held. As personal telegrapher and assistant to Thomas Scott of the Pennsylvania Railroad, Carnegie studied railroad operations in depth in order to understand everything that went on around him. He made himself so needed that when Scott was promoted, Carnegie replaced him as superintendent of the Western Division. From that position, he began to see possibilities that lured him into the iron and steel business where he made his fortune.

Carnegie made steady, disciplined progress that eventually led to sensational success. Instead of thinking in terms of miracles or even unexpected breakthroughs, he was constantly alert for ways to use what he had learned to move on to the next step.

At the heart of Carnegie's attitude was curiosity and a willingness to develop himself. In my view, development means taking responsibility for learning, building and using abilities and skills in order to advance on the basis of performance.

Self-Development Is an Important Key

Most magnet people are like Andrew Carnegie—willing to learn whatever is needed to reach a goal. Originally a financial analyst, Stephanie DiMarco taught herself programming when she founded Advent Software so that she could talk about programming authoritatively with prospective customers. The more knowledge she demonstrated, the more receptive her customers were.

Chicago Tribune founder Joseph Medill taught himself journalism by hanging around a local newspaper and absorbing whatever he could about setting type, using a press, writing editorials, and interviewing people. Grammy award winner Paul Simon learned the music industry from the inside by singing for other songwriters, producing songs for other bands, and watching what happened in the studio and the publishing house. Immersing himself in many musical styles also paid off in hit records inspired by reggae and other global rhythms. To polish his communication skills, Winston Churchill read world history and traveled extensively to learn about various world affairs and modeled his letter and speech writing on the best examples he could find. The talents he honed later proved powerful in boosting England's morale during World War II.

Opening yourself to self-development requires humility. Know-it-alls let pride shut themselves off from the need to improve. That's a lesson jockey Kent Desormeaux learned painfully. Already a top jockey at 25, he let fame go to his head and developed a reputation for arrogance and laziness among trainers and owners. When they stopped hiring him, he realized he had to start over...at the bottom. He put aside his pride and started mucking the stalls, grooming and feeding horses, and listening to others for their insights into racing techniques. Back in the saddle, he analyzed his own form and worked on his manners. His hard work paid off when he rode Fusaichi Pegasus to victory in the 2000 Kentucky Derby—but he still strives to learn all he can about racing by reading the Racing Form to learn the competition and watching films and TV monitors to analyze and anticipate what competing jockeys do.

Take a tip from these examples and learn from the experts around you. Magnet people don't simply arrive at their position overnight. Everyone has something to share about their journey. Don't be standoffish—get to know the people you admire and ask for their advice. Probe for their good decisions as well as their false turns, and follow their example to avoid making the same mistakes yourself.

Immerse yourself in your subject. Learn more than anyone else and you'll become the person to whom others defer...automatically putting you in a position of leadership.

But don't get *too* narrow! The problems of today's world are too complex for one discipline to answer. Strive to be a renaissance person who supplements expertise in one area with proficiency in many others. Above all, don't hoard your knowledge. Knowledge should lead to collaboration and engender a willingness to share what you know.

Finally, when you're leading other people, remember that they need to practice self-development, too. When people stop learning, they stop growing. When they stop growing, they get bored. And when they get bored, they may leave—a big problem for knowledge-based businesses!

When you find good people, keep them growing by making sure they are constantly broadening their skills. Reward employees not just for how much they add to the bottom line but for their willingness to absorb and share knowledge. Integrity and trustworthiness, as Chapter 1 noted, will foster loyalty. Creating opportunities for continual learning is another ingredient in the recipe. Set the example by committing to your own continual self-development, and seal the bond by providing for others to do the same.

Ready to develop, or to encourage others to do so? Follow these ten principles of adult learning:

1. Adult learners must have a desire to learn and a purpose for their learning.
2. Adult learners have practical learning needs.
3. Adult learners respond to concrete ideas and tasks.
4. Adult learning is rooted in the accumulated experience of the learner.
5. Adult learners may have to discard previous learning.
6. Adult learning depends on the physical condition of the learner.
7. Adult learners often lack confidence in their ability to learn.
8. Adult learning often depends on the personality of the learner.
9. Adult learning is most effective when learners can proceed at their own pace.
10. Adult learning is more effective when learners are involved in the evaluation of their own learning.

The difference between a top-notch athlete and an Olympic athlete is only about 10 percent. Giving 10 percent more than the next person can compound like interest very quickly.

Get Up One More Time

Magnet people don't go down for the count the first time they encounter turbulence. Nor do they give up the second. The fifth. Or the twenty-seventh.

This kind of persistence is easiest to see in people who have overcome physical disabilities. When women's soccer star Michelle Akers was diagnosed with Chronic Fatigue Immune Dysfunction Syndrome in 1991, she worked hard to hide it. On the field, she would play hard, train diligently, and try to appear normal. Off the field, overcome by fatigue, blurred vision, and poor balance and coordination, she would crawl into her bed. But she didn't stay there. By making changes in her diet and carefully budgeting her energy, she began to overcome CFIDS and was able to return to soccer with the 1999 Women's World's Cup Championship Team.

Runner John Register was training for the 1996 Olympic Games when he landed the wrong way after clearing a hurdle and severed an artery behind his left knee. The new amputee devoted himself to a tough rehabilitation regimen that included walking, weight lifting, and swimming. He quickly progressed from 50 yards to a mile of laps and eventually swam the anchor leg of the 4 x 100-meter medley relay in the 1996 Paralympic Games in Atlanta, helping the U.S. team finish fifth.

Watching runners at the Paralympic Games rekindled his determination to run. Almost four years after his accident, he hit the track. Plagued by balance problems, he found a better, more flexible prosthesis that gave him more control. Steady progress earned him a place on the U.S. disabled-track-and-field team in the 2000 Paralympic Games in Sydney.

"It's not what happens to you. It's what you do about it," says W. Mitchell (who uses only his first name initial), an author, TV host, and professional speaker. Mitchell was severely burned in a motorcycle accident and left without hands. He had finally recovered and started a new business when he received an even bigger blow: he was paralyzed in an airplane accident.

But even then he didn't give up. He pulled himself out of his post-accident depression and dedicated himself to exercise and therapy. Slowly, painfully, what had appeared impossible became a little less painful as he copes with the world from a wheelchair and dedicates himself to overcoming new obstacles.

Broadcaster and former pro-basketball star Bill Walton had to overcome a terrible speech impediment before he could become the relaxed, confident broadcaster he is today. Laughed out of a speech class at UCLA, he began to practice speaking and communicating just as he practiced basketball. Daily exercises and drills to strengthen his jaw muscles and smooth his speech paid off.

Getting up all over again takes guts, determination, and flexibility. If you can't make it work one way, try another. Change the rules, or invent new ones.

When Bernie Marcus and Arthur Blank founded Home Depot, they faced skepticism from investors and suppliers. But they persisted, and eventually found people willing to back them and vendors willing to work with them. "We were always pushing boundaries beyond where our industry's conventional wisdom suggested we could go," they remember. When one avenue was blocked, they sought another. Their enduring faith in their own judgment eventually prevailed as they shaped their concept of a home improvement warehouse with the lowest prices, best selection, and best service into nearly 800 stores and $30 billion in sales.

Tales of people who came back from failure inspire again and again. One of my personal favorites is the story of Brenda Faye Butler. The single mother of two on welfare had a vision after her third child was stillborn. Lying in the hospital, still stunned from what had happened, she reflected on her life and decided it was time to change.

Brenda Faye didn't like the example she was setting for her daughters. She didn't want her legacy to them to be a life cycle of poverty and struggle.

First, she studied for her high school equivalency exam—not very difficult, since she had been only two credits short of graduation when she left. With that behind her, she enrolled at Chicago State University, taking classes while her children were in school. Five years later she graduated and became a teacher on Chicago's southwest side. Today she owns a home, manages her own checking and savings account, and belongs to an investment club.

In reflecting on her journey, she quotes Frederick Douglass: "If there is no struggle, there is no progress."

Besides getting up one more time, magnet people also complete what they start. Ever heard of John Stephen Akhwari? During the 1968 Mexico City Olympics, the Tanzanian marathon runner crossed the finish line bloodied and bandaged an hour after everyone else. Asked why he stuck with the race even though the winner had been declared, he said, "My country did not send me to Mexico City to start the race. They sent me to finish."

All of these people gave their best—even when they didn't win. No matter how trying the circumstances, how grinding the pain, how discouraging the odds, they committed themselves to finishing the job and doing their best.

Magnet people keep going even when the work is dull, repetitive, but just plain necessary. Plenty of people fight for the glamorous work. But only magnet people stay late to stuff envelopes—always with their vision in mind.

Michael Dell, for example, plugged away for years before he was able to reshape the personal computer supply chain to support his direct sales methods. He was so committed to the business he started in his dorm room that he hid his inventory in the bathtub when his parents came to persuade him to complete his degree instead of running a company. His persistence paid off. Today his parents are convinced, the computer industry has been changed by his business, and he is one of the richest men in the world!

"All things come to those who wait...
but only what is left over
by those who hustle."

—Abraham Lincoln

The future is not the result of choices among alternatives, nor is it a place we are going. It is a condition we are creating. The paths to it are not found but made. The activity of making those paths changes both the maker and the destination.

A Study in Diligence: Edward O. Wilson

If there's anybody I think represents diligence, it's biologist Edward O. Wilson. Again and again, he has turned adversity into success.

Wilson had plenty of good reasons to succumb to hardship. His father committed suicide when he was young. Partially blind and deaf and small for his age, what few friendships he made were interrupted each time his family moved.

Instead of feeling sorry for himself, he challenged himself with new goals. He successfully tackled a 420-customer paper route, earned many badges in Boy Scouts, became an Eagle Scout, and worked hard to build a career from his love of nature.

When his book *Sociobiology* was published, it stirred up controversy. His provocative hypothesis was that some behaviors of animals and humans might be biologically based. Accused of racism, fascism, and sexism, he was even showered with a pitcher of ice water during a speech. Once again, instead of being discouraged by the public outcry, he resolved to meet it. Realizing he had only thought about his theories from the scientific point of view, he began to study the beliefs of his adversaries in order to understand and address their objections. When his next book, *On Human Nature*, was published in 1979, it won the Pulitzer Prize for general nonfiction. And his opponents were silenced.

Wilson's advice: "Most people take it too easy when they go in the field. They follow the trails and walk a short distance into the woods…you should walk in a straight line through the forest. Try to go over any barrier you meet. It's hard, but that's the best way."

Diligence Doesn't Mean Fanaticism

Hard work isn't beneficial when it's taken too far and leads to burnout.

Heed the stories of people who have collapsed under the weight of their own ambition, and give yourself a break now and then. Don't just keep piling on the pressure.

Alex Gibbs, former offensive line coach of the Denver Broncos, believed he became addicted to coaching the same way others get addicted to cigarettes or alcohol. "I would literally go six months and never see my neighbors," he said when he resigned. "I would live there and wouldn't ever see them. I'd leave before they were up and I'd be home after they were in bed…I have a sickness with achievement, I have a sickness with pressure, I have a sickness of trying to be successful. I was going to fall. It was just a matter of time."

Everyone knows somebody who has carried ambition too far.

Magnet people don't drive themselves to sickness in a compulsion to succeed. They know how to care for themselves and achieve a sustainable balance. They treat themselves as carefully and respectfully as they treat their best friend. They don't berate themselves when things go wrong. They look for what's wrong before they look for who's wrong, and they try to anticipate problems rather than stay depressed over failure.

Set goals, focus your efforts, and work hard—but take time for yourself. Read a book. Take a walk. Enjoy your friends and family. Don't abuse your most important relationships by working too many hours. Stop. Relax. Rejuvenate. Or you'll be too exhausted, emotionally and physically, to achieve anything at all.

In building his company and his fortune, Goodyear Tire founder Franklin A. Seiberling sought a balance between business and leisure. He should know. After losing millions in the Panic of 1920, Seiberling poured $18 million of his own money into Goodyear rather than declare bankruptcy. Forced out of the company in 1921, he went on to found another company, Seiberling Rubber Company, which became part of Firestone in 1964. But while his determination to keep his businesses running never faltered, he did not make his personal life the price of his success.

"I do not mean that the business should not receive close attention, but it should not get it all," he said. "There should be close attention to health. Had I lost my health and retained my millions, I would have been bankrupt."

Some Thoughts on Time

Take time to...

Think — it is the source of self-renewal.

Play — it will keep you young.

Read — it will rejuvenate your mind.

Worship-it is the acknowledgment of your limitations.

Help others — it will return more than you give.

Show love — it is the key to life's greatest

satisfactions.

Daydream — it will provide a road map for your

future.

Laugh — it is the secret to restoring your balance.

Work on new skills — it will keep you in demand.

Plan — it will determine whether you have time for

the first nine!

Chapter 3

Magnet People Are Objective

What are the facts?

Where is the evidence?

Why should I believe you?

When it's time to solve a problem, make a decision, or implement a change, these are the questions magnet people ask. They want facts first. After facts are in hand, they welcome opinions, judgments, and impressions.

This does not mean that magnet people are automatons who value reason alone. On the contrary. They are ready and willing to consider the social, political, emotional, and relationship aspects of a decision—once they have the evidence. But before they start down the track, they want to know whether they are dealing with a mountain or a molehill.

Besides examining evidence carefully, they also listen carefully. They surround themselves with people who speak freely, ethically, honestly. No "yes men" here! They know that selecting people whose only function is to agree will not lead to the best decision. They want to be influenced toward the *best* decision, not the one that might be most politically acceptable.

Magnet people work toward the best possible decisions because they concentrate on ideas, projects, and relationships that will outlive them. This chapter looks at four ways they make those decisions and ensure that legacy:

- Don't look back
- Look for what's wrong before who's wrong
- Value performance over seniority
- Ignore entitlements and earn everything

First-rate people hire first-rate people; second-rate people hire third-rate people.

—Leo Rosten

Don't Look Back

To me, "don't look back" means "don't get stuck in the past."

History *is* important—but historical thinking prevents individuals and organizations from adapting to new challenges and changes.

Magnet people have an appreciation for the past, and they use it to stay focused on the present and the future. They know that our personal and organizational histories reveal much about our strengths, weaknesses, accomplishments, values, priorities, and potential. They know it can help predict how one person will treat another, and what will be expected in a relationship.

But they don't let the past trap them.

Hewlett-Packard CEO Carly Fiorina is a fine example. Hewlett-Packard values its history so much that it employs a full-time archivist to care for its 60 years of artifacts. Even the garage where the company was started is a shrine to would-be entrepreneurs! But instead of letting the company rest on its distinguished laurels, Fiorina is prompting HP staff to focus on a world in which technological change is faster than ever.

Like Columbus, Fiorina and her executives steer by the stars.

As he left charted waters, Columbus shared his approach to navigation with his sailors. He knew it was impossible to set a course by watching the ever-changing waves. "A wise captain charts his course by a star which does not move," he said. "When your journey is long and the way before you is rough, never take your eyes off the North Star. Focus your vision on beautiful, unwavering, constant 'Polaris.'"

Don't make decisions by looking at the waves. Chart your course according to fixed stars—principles and values you hold dear and that will sustain you through good times and bad.

You can't set a course by looking behind you. Value your history, but don't carry old baggage. Travel light. Within firm moral and ethical boundaries, be flexible. Be prepared to adjust and adapt as change requires.

Don't let your history get in the way of your future.

"Ideals are like the stars. We will never reach them, but like the mariners on the sea, we chart our course by them."

—Carl Schurz

Focus on What's Wrong, Not Who's Wrong

If you're always looking for somebody to blame, you will be successful 100 percent of the time.

But you won't solve the problem.

Problems are an inevitable part of life. What distinguishes the magnet person from others is how problems are tackled.

Magnet people aren't afraid to deal with reality. In fact, they want to. When a problem crops up, they acknowledge it. If they need information, they ask for it. Instead of getting sidetracked by who triggered the problem, they stay focused on creating solutions.

Too many people play the "blame game." They look at *who* is wrong, not *what* is wrong. It's easy to see this attitude in the growing epidemic of workplace incivility.

Disrespectful behavior is all around us. Bosses shout and insult...accuse staff or colleagues of being ignorant...undermine their credibility in front of others...even send nasty, demeaning notes—just like kids in junior high school!

Not only do these tactics fail to solve problems, they cause incalculable damage in the workplace.

What happens to a person after being subjected to this kind of behavior? A study by Professor Christine Pearson of the Kenan-Flagler Business School at the University of North Carolina discovered that:

- 28 percent lost work time avoiding the instigator
- 53 percent lost work time worrying about the incident or future interactions
- 37 percent felt their commitment to the organization declined
- 22 percent decreased their effort at work
- 10 percent decreased the amount of time they spent at work
- 46 percent contemplated changing jobs to avoid the instigator
- 12 percent actually changed jobs to avoid the instigator.

What a waste of energy—energy that could be devoted to solving the underlying problems.

In half of these incidents—which mostly took place in generally polite workplaces where people tended to treat each other with respect—the instigator had yelled or shouted and attempted to flaunt his or her status at the target.

That's simply inexcusable. You don't make yourself great by showing how small someone else is!

To attack this serious and growing problem, a company called Envisionworks developed an Organization Civility Index (OCI)^{SM}. It is a brief survey completed by employees that provides an accurate measure of the nature, frequency and costs of workforce incivility. Based on extensive research at the University of North Carolina, it has proven to be effective in:

- reducing the risk of employee-generated litigation
- improving recruiting success
- decreasing employee turnover
- increasing productivity.

There are a lot of loose cannons out there. You've seen them. I've seen them. Some are extremely talented people. But, "Out-of-control emotions can make smart people stupid," says Daniel Goleman in his landmark book, *Emotional Intelligence.*

With little empathy, self-control, and discipline, these "smart people" are rude to peers and disrespectful of staff. They are temperamental, hard to get along with, respond to problems emotionally and are sore losers.

Worse yet, some of them are extremely powerful—which often leads to staff making excuses for them. This compounds the problem because no one should make excuses for people at the top, or look the other way when a bully is raging.

People want to be shown how to correct mistakes. But they don't want their mistakes corrected in public. They expect remedial actions and most prefer a supervisor who is fair, firm—and tactful.

When Aon Corporation approached Ryan Insurance about a merger, W. Clement Stone—then in his 80s—said he would still run the company and would keep Patrick Ryan, Chair of the other company, around to "train."

"I could have been a bully and embarrassed Stone in front of management," said Ryan. Instead he called a special board meeting and asked the board to communicate the boundaries of Stone's role. Stone eventually left the board in 1990.

True magnet people use their influence not to bully but to influence an organization's behavior from the top. They establish behavior expectations at the highest levels and then follow them to the letter. In this way, many wasteful interpersonal problems are avoided and energy can be directed toward tackling the real problem.

Follow the example of magnet people, and work out conflicts maturely. Stay focused on the situation, not the people. And seek to create solutions, not more problems.

Steps to Solving Problems

I recommend these seven steps to solving problems.

Step one: Acknowledge the problem. Don't hide bad news! Problems that remain hidden won't be solved.

Step two: Ask the right questions. Seek the information needed to untangle a problem or do a job. And ask the right questions, not the wrong ones.

Wrong Question — Who got us into this mess?

Right Question — What do you recommend?

Wrong Question — Should we ask John or Sue?

Right Question — What is the right step?

Step three: Look for facts, not opinions. If people think they can get by with giving you opinions before they have to deliver facts, they'll give opinions first every time. You need data, evidence, documentation. Examine opinions in light of these facts. Considering opinions before facts is a fatal flaw! There will be plenty of time to view points and sentiments.

Step four: Ignore excuses. When a problem surfaces, don't waste time arguing about the validity of excuses. Ignore the excuses, and stay focused on the problem. If someone says that interruptions prevented her from finishing a job, don't ask, "Why did you let them interrupt you?" Instead, respond with, "Fine. What is the status of the job now, and when will you be finished?"

Step five: Delegate. It sounds paradoxical, but you gain authority by giving it away.

When a problem arises, give the people it concerns and affects personally the opportunity to solve it first. People directly involved have greater knowledge of the factors causing the problem. They also have a vested interest—a sense of proprietorship and accomplishment—in seeing the solution work. They are no longer being handed solutions to their problems; they are determining their course of action. They will usually devise better solutions. Listen to their advice closely!

Step six: Solve the right problem, not the wrong one. Don't be disappointed if your first idea doesn't work. Think in terms of a sequence of steps to be climbed one at a time. Write them down. Accomplish the first and the second will look easier.

Step seven: Stick to it. Even massive problems can be solved little by little!

Coaches often have a very practical approach to solving problems, which occur continually in games and must be solved immediately. "Whenever I have major changes that need to be made," says Duke University top-rated basketball coach Mike Krzyzewski, "I look at what we have and say, 'Let's figure out how we're going to do it.'" The roots of his can-do approach lie in his optimism, learned from his years in military academy. "If it's sunny or muddy or whatever, you figure out a way to win. If you spend any time being pessimistic, then you're an idiot."

Why Problems Aren't Solved

- Staff often will not criticize supervisors.
- People tend to be self-protective of their positions and hopes for advancement.
- The presence of people with technical expertise tends to intimidate those who are afraid of admitting ignorance.
- A sense of urgency tends to stimulate unreliable judgments.
- Personal conflicts often work against constructive, cooperative problem solving.
- People see problems from their own viewpoint rather than a broader organization perspective.
- Focusing on a distasteful situation clouds the atmosphere with tension, fear, and often uncertainty for both parties.

A man may fail many times,

but he isn't a failure until

he begins to blame somebody else.

—J. Paul Getty

Is the Problem Miscommunication?

When a shipment doesn't go out when it should have...when agreed-upon actions aren't taken...when follow-up with customers doesn't occur...the reason is more often miscommunication than neglect.

Language is susceptible to misinterpretation. People seldom say what they mean. For evidence that people talk or write before they think, look no further than your voice mail or e-mail messages!

That problem is only compounded by our tendency to be "lazy listeners" who do not bring our attention and skill to listening. We let our minds wander.

But miscommunication can be silent...until a problem crops up. Until that shipment is overlooked, no one realizes that the instructions were unclear or ignored.

If you realize that you miscommunicated, it takes little effort and less time to clarify matters and fix the problem.

Anticipate the possibility of misunderstanding and do what you can to avert it. Hone your listening skills. They will let you surmount many pitfalls of human communication and become more effective.

Listen with your mind and heart
as well as your ears.

Value Performance Over Seniority

If ever there was a sacred cow, it's seniority.

Too many people pull rank in the face of challenges. They consider themselves too senior to put out a fire, or even to take the heat. They dismiss themselves from tasks they see as too menial.

Seniority often goes hand in hand with experience. But what *is* experience, really? The dictionary says. "Facts or events observed... direct participation in events."

With that definition in mind, consider the difference between the "possibility viewpoints" and enthusiasm expressed by kindergarten children as contrasted with college students. If you ask kindergarten children, "Can you draw? Sing? Dance?" they will all say yes. Ask "Will you show me?" and they all will. Ask college students and most will say no and the few who say yes will have qualifications.

Experience *can* diminish. Too many of us allow experience to limit our lives somewhere between the ages of 5 and 20. And what we call growing up really amounts to shrinking down!

Unfortunately, the same thing happens in the work place. Too many people, instead of growing and improving, become less and less motivated to increase their effectiveness. They want to just get by and have pay raises be automatic.

We need to change our values. Experience and seniority can be good—*if* they can be applied to solving *current* problems. Knowledge and position alone are useless. That's why true professionals—magnet leaders in the making—are committed to self-development and lifelong learning. They are comfortable being judged by what they finish, not what they attempt. And far from being threatened by talent, they recognize competence in others and use these talents to supplement and complement their own work.

These people don't mistake rank, salary, seniority, privileges or even ownership for leadership. Owners who think they can buy loyalty are not leaders. Respect cannot be bought. It must be earned.

When magnet people surround themselves with people who are better than they are, they are clearly saying that they value performance over seniority... that getting the job done is more important than standing on ceremony.

Just ask Ned Thomson of Thomson Shore Printers. Never mind that he was the company's co-founder and leader. When a shipment of books needed to be driven from the Dexter, Michigan plant to Columbus, Ohio, Ned took the wheel and drove all night in a snowstorm. So many cartons of books filled the van that there was barely enough space left for Ned. In Columbus, he carried carton after carton down a cellar stairway with little help from the customer.

Ned's partner Harry Shore drove a large, rented truck full of books to Durham, North Carolina, during the oil embargo of 1974, when lines were long and many customers could only buy 5 gallons of gas at a time—just about what the truck got per mile. To make the trip, Harry stopped and waited in line at every station he passed, and coasted down every hill he could. The tank was never more than ¼ full—but he got the books there on time.

MORAL: *only results matter.* Experience, seniority, competence, good intentions, even ownership—all are insignificant without results.

Getting results entails four simple steps:
1. Delegate
2. Support
3. Measure
4. Reward.

What is accomplished is more important than what is promised.

Someone once defined the manager, only half in jest, as that person who sees the visitors so that everyone else can get the work done.

—H. Mintzberg

Delegate Responsibility

It's impossible to know what others can do when you try to do everything yourself. That's why effective delegation is so basic in building an organization.

Ron Harris, CEO of Pervasive Software Inc., knows this well. He has pushed delegation to new levels. When he asks an employee to take over a major project or product, he appoints them as internal CEO. Each one receives the resources, cash, and people to achieve the goal, along with authority for sales, development and marketing. Harris' unique approach to empowerment has reduced the time it takes Pervasive Software to introduce new products and complete special projects.

Sadly, many people fail to delegate — and contrive elaborate excuses for not sharing power and authority. Among the most frequent alibis:

This job is so important that only I can do it

I like doing the job myself

I can do this work better than anyone else

If I delegate to others, what will I do?

Several factors are behind these excuses. Some people are so anxious to "prove themselves" that they refuse to delegate. Others are motivated by inadequacy: they fear being shown up by someone else. Rigidity—the conviction that nothing can be done properly unless done personally—is another factor. So is impatience: "It takes longer to explain than to do myself."

Some of the worst offenders are recently promoted managers. Still uncomfortable in their new position, they give into the irresistible urge to go back and tell their replacements what to do. Others are so attached to some aspect of the job they can't bear to delegate it.

In the end, delegation requires trust and faith in others. A great manager invites others to come and work and promises to help them be as successful as possible. Great managers let people grow, take care to assign them to the right roles, and want people to succeed. They try to draw out qualities that are already in people, instead of trying to put in what isn't there. Effective delegation happens when a manager understands a person's unique qualities, can help make the most of them and deliver great results.

Andrew Carnegie used delegation to build one of the largest conglomerates of the 19th century. He believed that a good executive didn't hold the reins of day-to-day management. Instead, he felt his job was to install reliable employees and reliable systems, and let the employees manage their own affairs. He turned to expert scientists to ensure that his blast furnaces operated at maximum efficiency, and top accountants to institute accurate cost-accounting measures.

But he didn't leave everything up to his employees. When an important contract was being negotiated, he attended the closing and stayed until he could take home the written agreement.

Knowin' it ain't the same as doin' it.

—Old Hoosier saying

Great leaders gain authority by giving it away.

—Admiral James B. Stockdale

Support Your Team

Magnet people don't demand results in a vacuum. Because they know their success as a leader is directly related to the success of their team, they look for and hire the best—and then nurture and motivate their performers. They expect excellence. They know what motivates people. They know how to get the best efforts. They understand individual strengths and weaknesses. They provide ongoing training and make training a substantial part of budgets. They decide what people need most to become more productive. **Most of all, they want people to succeed**.

National Football League Commissioner Pete Rozelle was supportive, pleasant, and polite to everyone—so people relaxed around him, and took him at his word. His calm manner and even temper created a win-win atmosphere that earned him friends and helped him meet his goals for the NFL.

"The coach's challenge is to motivate each player in such a way that he performs at his best while helping the team perform at its best," says Duke's Krzyzewski. He tailors his support to meet the needs of each player, offering words of encouragement, challenges, or quips. In exchange for his support, he expects his players to commit to meeting high standards of excellence.

Teamwork begins when you start to think about what others need and how you can help them. Outside the locker room, teamwork can be expressed through mentoring. Alan Cole, an outstanding trainer and Human Resources professional, remembers the support of a boss who worked with him every day to increase his knowledge and proficiency. "He went well beyond the norm," says Cole. "He put a lot of his personal time and effort into my education. He wrote out quizzes for me, reviewed procedures, discussed what and how, and showed me many things about systems and procedures in Air Force nuclear missile operations." Another boss prepared him for meetings by explaining what he was going to say and why, and then debriefed the results with him afterwards.

The ultimate in support can be found at Lucky Dogs, the New Orleans company whose 10-foot-long hotdog-shaped carts are driven by vendors whose backgrounds are checkered with alcoholism and prison records and whose work habits leave a lot to be desired. To manage this unlikely workforce, general manager Jerry Strahan relies on patience and flexibility. While he enforces a few simple rules and draws the line at theft, he is always ready to lend a helping hand and often forgives and forgets infractions. Lucky Dogs is profitable, and Strahan is viewed as a great mediator and father figure by its down-at-the-heels workers.

Make people responsible for their work rather than their job...their achievements rather than their objectives...and their potential rather than their goals.

—Thomas Faranda

Measure Results

Results only happen when expectations are clear.

To create a climate of success, clearly define the results expected of individuals, as well as the measures to be applied in judging those results. Use objectives and action plans to make sure everyone understands *who* will do *what* by *when*.

Then evaluate progress and reward performance accordingly.

When expectations are unclear, you will get involved in tugs of war about what you meant and what your intentions were; whether failure occurred or a situation was just not explained adequately. If you don't define performance upfront, you will constantly haggle and hassle.

Define what is important, and you will get it. Measure it, and it will get better. What gets measured, gets done! Measurable goals will make it easier, when problems arise, to see what's wrong instead of who's wrong.

You do not lead by hitting people over the head. That's assault, not leadership.

—Dwight D. Eisenhower

Reward Performers

To benefit most from the example set by magnet people:

- Always favor the performers. Let everyone know who is getting the biggest rewards.
- Never favor mediocrity. When you do, you are vulnerable to losing your best people because they will think you can't tell the difference between the best and the worst.
- Don't retain people who don't perform. Keep only performers.

It isn't difficult to find out who isn't performing. Coworkers can tell you. So will customers. When you find out who isn't performing, take action.

This can be a tough lesson to learn—especially for tenderhearted people. Paul Orfalea, founder of Kinko's, couldn't bring himself to fire a manager who lied and stole money because the manager said expenses connected with his father's heart attack had driven him to steal. But his leniency upset managers who *had* followed the rules. Not until Orfalea realized that his unwillingness to take action had compromised the working environment at several stores did he understand that he couldn't let his heart rule his mind. Next time the manager stole, Orfalea fired him.

His lesson? "The hardest thing to do as the leader in this business is to hurt people's feelings, but sometimes you have to."

A Piece of the Action

Magnet people are usually not laid back and easy going nor are they "popular" because they seek to be or need to be. Rather they attract followers and retain loyalty because they have a strong commitment to the people they depend upon.

Here's a good example. Bob Thompson was, until July 18, 1999, owner of Michigan's largest asphalt and paving company, Thompson McCully. On that day he sold the company for $422 million.

Thompson started the business in 1959 with $3500 which his wife Ellen had earned as a substitute teacher. According to employees, he was a tough taskmaster who pushed people hard six days a week and frequently pitched in himself with a road crew.

So what did Bob Thompson do with the proceeds from selling his company? He gave a third of it, $128 million, to his 550 employees. Ninety of them became instant millionaires. Why? "When you see the pain and suffering those around you have gone through with you, you realize everybody should get a piece of the action. That's what America should be all about," he says.

With that outlook, it's no wonder so many people made such great sacrifices for so long with not a hint of his big payoff.

Thompson's explanation for the gift is simple. "I've got a big ego," he says, "but this was just the right thing to do."

Loyalty is important and it works both ways. One way to think of loyalty is in terms of those employees who have yet to receive a better offer. In other words, the best employees know they can always make good money. What they want is respect—to be trusted, given freedom, listened to. And they also want to give respect—they won't stay at a company that doesn't measure up to their standards of excellence and honor.

Magnet people consider how every decision will affect the attitudes of the best employees. Every corner cut, every customer chiseled, takes a nick out of loyalty. The best employees are always learning how to be better people...and when necessary, WHERE to be better people.

Ignore Entitlements, Earn Everything

I hate entitlement.

People who feel they are entitled to something for whatever reason—seniority, race, gender, family background, education—are only hurting themselves. In my experience, there is no equal sign between seniority and performance—or any kind of entitlement and performance.

Yet we live in an age marked by entitlement as the siren song of many politicians. I think it's crippling.

I attribute my success to this:
I never gave or took an excuse.

—Florence Nightingale

Life is not always easy. It isn't about quotas or privilege or "soft landings". **There's nothing we really "deserve" except opportunity.** The only success that lasts comes from hard work and discipline.

The expectation that things should be easy or that we can accomplish things without hard work and sacrifice saps the will and dulls initiative and productivity. It can also lead us to look for the easy way—the short cut—when what we need to do is establish the diligence of working for what we believe to be truly important.

Not taking the easy way is part of what gave two-time Tour de France winner Lance Armstrong his victories. At one time, he made his living by winning one-day European classic races. But when he decided to win the Tour de France, he stopped participating. Instead of trying to win every race, he focused on one or two. Trained carefully. And did everything he could to achieve his big goal.

His long-term view worked—not only in his battle for the Tour de France, but his battle against cancer.

Winners can defer gratification.

Losers want it NOW.

As one of the most prosperous businessmen in the United States, industrialist Andrew W. Mellon could have accustomed himself to special treatment. But his sense of humility led him to set aside entitlement. Summoned to Ohio to discuss a position in President-elect Warren Harding's administration, he walked a mile to Harding's home when no one met him at the train station, and waited patiently for his audience instead of accepting offers to go to the head of the line.

Instead of being content with a reputation as a great power forward, basketball player Karl Malone continually challenges himself to improve his performance on the court. The headlines are full of athletes who indulge in the perks of celebrity...but Malone stays focused on an exercise routine that strengthens his muscles and cardiovascular system and has built his endurance and will. Staying in better shape than his opponents has made the game easier for him. Through his work he has upgraded every facet of his game and after 16 years in the NBA, still believes there is room for improvement.

The four vital sources of strength are love, prayer, unselfishness and accountability. The basic causes of weakness are entitlement, excuses, selfishness, and blame.

Don't Just Earn...Give!

Those who are most satisfied with life—who achieve a strong sense of meaning and fulfillment—often find their answer by focusing their lives on values and in service towards something larger than themselves.

Happiness and balance are not goals but the byproducts of a life based on deeply held values and a firm foundation of truth. They come not from seeking merely what they want but from living a life of service and stewardship. LONG-TERM SUCCESS IS MORE ABOUT SERVICE THAN ABOUT SELF. Happiness comes from using gifts to accomplish worthy goals. Using talents and gifts for others gives life richness and depth.

Balance comes from knowing what is truly important, doing those things, and dropping the activities that don't really matter.

Measure your wealth by what you'd have left if you lost all your money.

Chapter 4

Magnet People Are Unselfish

Remember the phrase, "no man is an island?"

Magnet people never forget it. They know they didn't achieve their success on their own. They always remember and appreciate the people behind the scenes who helped them.

Greatness is not sought. It is the outcome of unselfish acts to benefit others. Unselfishness is a key characteristic of magnet people. They are concerned not merely with earning a living but in serving people who need them. Tyrants, on the other hand, are not great. They are small people whose concern with themselves is disguised as favors. Magnet people appreciate the benefits they have received from others, and feel an obligation to contribute in return.

In searching for magnet people these four qualities stand out:

- They listen mostly to those who love them
- They instinctively share credit
- They change before they have to
- They use everything they have.

When you get to the mountaintop,

be prepared to answer this question:

"Who did you bring with you?"

In this chapter, you'll see why magnet people can single out the best voices to listen to. Why they are so quick to share credit and recognize others. How they plan for change, and martial resources for their work.

Listen First to Those Who Love You

We all need at least one "prompter" whose advice is consistently reliable, who we can fall back on in a crisis, whose perspective we can trust when decisions need to be made, and who can help us be objective.

But in a world crowded with competing voices, it's easy to listen to the wrong ones. Like someone who doesn't have your best interests at heart. Or someone who may tempt you with a solution that looks easy but will only create turmoil and heartache.

How can you know which voice to trust? My advice: Listen most closely to those who love you.

If you listen to just anyone, "you find out very quickly that you're the only one who cares about your vision," says a seasoned entrepreneur.

Does this mean you shouldn't necessarily listen to others' suggestions? Certainly not. In Chapter 5 we'll talk about the great value of constructive criticism.

The bedrock notion here is to differentiate sharply between the advice and views of those who truly will feel your pain if you fail versus those who say they will but are glad you and not they are on the "hot seat."

Gladys Hampton was in a position to truly feel the pain when her husband, jazz vibraphonist Lionel Hampton, appointed her his business manager in the 1940s. With her husband's interests in mind, Gladys Hampton negotiated contracts and royalties with record companies, invested his earnings carefully, and kept Hampton and his band on a tight budget.

Other men laughed at Hampton for letting a woman run his business, but it was Hampton who had the last laugh. During his long career many musicians rose to prominence and then faded away. Their short careers made managers, agents, and record producers rich…but often left the musicians themselves bankrupt. Thanks to Gladys, Hampton prospered. "She was the keynote to everything I did," Hampton said of his wife.

Tom Malone, president of Milliken & Company, tells a similar story. In college, he played football—but he wasn't very big, he wasn't very good, and he suffered many injuries. "When I tell people about it, they always ask me, 'Why did you keep doing it?'" he remembers. "For a long time I had no answer. Then one day it hit me. If there hadn't been any fans in the stands cheering me on—my family and friends—I wouldn't have kept on playing and trying so hard. But there were, so I did."

Always Share Credit

Magnet people never forget those who hold the ladder for them…and they ride to success on the shoulders of those they have helped.

Humble about their own accomplishments, they are eager to tout the achievements of others. While they accept credit when it is due, they share it liberally and without thinking, with those who helped them. Lyricist Ira Gershwin said of his brother George, "My job was to sit and listen to music that George created and then set words to it." Early in his career, he wrote under a pseudonym so that he wouldn't be accused of trying to capitalize on his brother's fame. And throughout his career he preferred talking about his brother to talking about himself.

Magnet people tend to hide their ego behind their need for measurable progress…and their need to see others succeed. They have great confidence in the people who follow them. By sharing responsibility and accountability, they give their people the tools to meet high standards. And by acknowledging achievement and sharing credit, they build the confidence needed to meet even higher goals.

Why, then, do so many people fail to share credit? Studies suggest that only half of those in management give adequate recognition for high performance and up to 40 percent of employees feel they *never* get recognized for outstanding performance. Many others feel they only attract the boss' attention when they have screwed up. Yet a Gallup Poll survey confirms that people who receive recognition and praise for good work are not only happier but more motivated and productive.

The consequences are easy to see: People want to receive credit for their work when they deserve it. Recognition is a big part of what gives meaning to a job. Inadequate acknowledgement, on the other hand, is a major cause of "flame out", especially for high achievers.

He who receives a good turn should never forget it; he who does one should never remember it.

The Secrets of Sharing Credit

All of us need to know that the work we do is important. Having our work validated publicly is one of the greatest sources of satisfaction we can have. Public or peer recognition answers our deep need to feel that we belong and are contributing to something worthwhile.

But all forms of recognition aren't equal. People want to be treated like individuals. An off-the-shelf, one-size-fits-all approach to praise and recognition looks indifferent or, worse, insincere. "You have all done a great job" does not have the same impact as, "We could not have done this without you, Jane."

To share credit effectively, find out what people want and tailor your praise to their expectations. Make recognition both public *and* personal. Above all, **if you don't mean it, don't say it!**

Plaques and gift certificates are great, but what really gets people excited is a personal thank you. A handwritten note from the company president creates a memento that can be revisited again and again. Public or social recognition like a party thrown to celebrate an accomplishment creates a memory that can last forever.

Appreciation is always appreciated.

Praise and recognition are difficult for some people. Expressing real appreciation means expressing real emotions in public, something many shy away from. When we put ourselves on the line to share how we feel about someone's performance or actions, we take a risk—and we're not always confident in our own skills as recognizers. The keys are honesty and sincerity.

Like any other skill, effective praise and recognition can be learned. Start small—perhaps with a compliment. Be specific, not general. Instead of saying, "I liked your report," say, "I liked your report so much I gave it directly to the president. The facts you dug up on the Jones case were right on target. I know he'll be impressed."

Look for ways to praise someone's character—perhaps their courage to stand up for a principle, or their levelheadedness during a crisis. Praise directed at character gets inside a person's self-image and self-worth. For example, "You are the only person I know in the company who could get such an unpopular viewpoint accepted."

Magnet people have overcome their hesitations and learned to praise without hesitation. People who are stingy with their praise get a stingy response and minimum effort when the chips are down.

The ambition of magnet people is not related to personal advancement or greed. It is based on involving others and their success.

Be creative in figuring out how to share credit. Keep in mind that people who are systematically encouraged and assisted in setting their own levels of achievement do significantly better than those who are not. And people who are praised when they reach those levels do best of all!

Finally, don't wait for a reason to acknowledge that someone else exists. Too many bosses distance themselves from the people around them, or do all their communicating through a formal chain of command. Break the chain. Say hello to people. Smile. Acknowledge a birthday. Saturn president Cynthia Trudell makes her presence known on the factory floor, stopping to inspect work, or visiting the break room to sing Happy Birthday to a Saturn team member. Advent Software co-founder Stephanie DiMarco keeps in constant touch with her employees and tries to make them feel that they are an important part of her company. Tom Heimsoth, Co-founder and Chairman of Resource Information Management Systems, enjoys finding out about employees' hobbies and families. All of these leaders go out of their way to show others that their presence is important.

Don't carve your name upon marble.
Carve it on hearts.

If you lead through fear you will have
little to respect; but if you lead through
respect you will have little to fear.

Don't Stop with Credit

Magnet people share a lot more than credit.

Neurosurgeon Dr. Ben Carson and his wife set up the Carson Scholars Fund with $500,000 of their own money. The fund provides college scholarships for academically talented students from the inner city.

Gilmore and Gold Reynolds were astute entrepreneurs who could have had anything in the world. Instead, they gave it all away to their hometown.

Partners in a wholesale snack-food business, the couple began selling bottled gas in 1946 in response to a boom in fuel-powered appliances. While their business and their stock market account flourished, they lived simply. They were so much like the folks next store that the first their neighbors learned of their wealth was after their death. The childless couple left $23 million to their community of Osgood, Indiana—more than the assessed value of every business and building in town. Now a foundation will dole out the money in $1 million annual grants for new sidewalks, an expanded library and YMCA, and other projects that benefit their town.

Gertrude Elion devoted her life to medical research that is saving thousands of lives. Among her major accomplishments—development of the first two drugs to successfully treat leukemia and the drug that makes organ transplants possible. She shared the Nobel Prize for physiology and medicine in 1988. Elion's core belief—"You must never feel you have failed. You can always come back and try later when you have more knowledge or better equipment and try again. I've done this and it worked." Yet with all her honors and accomplishments friends described her as "the most welcoming, approachable person they knew."

This kind of altruism is at the core of a magnet person's character. Studies show that altruists have loving parents who modeled selfless behavior, insisted on a strong moral code, and taught their children self-confidence. As a result, they have a strong sense that they can shape their destinies. They don't just think good thoughts. They think, "I can change things"—and like the Carsons, the Reynolds, and Gertrude Elion, that's exactly what they do.

I can live for two months
on a good compliment.

—Mark Twain

Manners Matter, Too

"People are not stepping stones to be walked on, used, and discarded," says author Lillian Glass, Ph.D.

Magnet people know this well. They make it a point to respect those around them. They know that if they respect others, they will be respected.

Sharing credit is one way to demonstrate respect. In effect, sharing credit means building bridges. "All work is social," says Lois P. Frankel, a business coach and senior partner at Corporate Coaching International. "Establishing good working relationships can help secure the cooperation of the people we need to accomplish our tasks. If we delay building good relationships until we really need them, it will be too late."

Among Frankel's tips for building respectful relationships:

1. Spend 10 minutes a day in casual conversation with someone in your organization.
2. Listen when people talk to you.
3. Ask for help when you need it.
4. Begin conversations with small talk. Don't just plunge into your agenda.
5. Be straightforward. Never let your desire to be liked "overshadow the need to make tough decisions."
6. Do favors for others.

Go even farther. Be courteous. Hold doors open. Greet people. Say goodbye when you finish a phone call instead of hanging up peremptorily. Say thank you, please, and pardon me. Magnet people never act like the world was created for their personal convenience!

The tongue is where the mind comes out in the open.

John Bogle, founder of the Vanguard Group mutual fund and one of the wealthiest and most respected men in that field, believes in treating everyone with respect, no matter where they are on the organization chart. He answers phones when needed and answers his own mail.

Jim Clark, a high school dropout, rebounded to start three companies, each valued at more than a billion dollars: Silicon Graphics, Netscape Communications and Healtheon Corporation. His focus is "to try to bring out the best in everyone." He tries to put his ego aside, surround himself with talented people, listen and let them teach him what he needs to know. We're not talking about courtesy here—or even empathy. **We're talking about a calculated, deliberate, persistent acknowledgment of what others can contribute and letting them do it.** Too many people who think of themselves as leaders get into serious trouble when they consistently superimpose their will and insist on their way.

Magnet people also know that no one deserves your best behavior more than your family. NFL linebacker Chris Spielman put aside his football career when his wife Stefanie was diagnosed with breast cancer. Sidelined by a neck injury, the former Detroit Lions player had planned to make a comeback with the Buffalo Bills. Instead, he stayed home with the couple's children and supported Stefanie through chemotherapy. "I knew in my heart it was the right thing to do," says Spielman. "We take our wedding vows very seriously." When Stefanie was declared cancer free, Spielman returned to his training; but when Stefanie's cancer returned and he retired from football in 2000, he again devoted time to caring for his family and to raising funds for cancer research.

The moral of these stories? As Jim Clark says, "It's amazing what you can gain merely by recognizing talent and how much you can lose by taking it for granted."

The Power of Example

If employees...

- Are constantly criticized, they will learn to blame others.
- Must deal with hostility and friction each day, they will become belligerent themselves.
- Are rarely commended, they will seek only routine duties.
- Frequently made to feel guilty, they will avoid difficult problems.
- Are allowed to make some mistakes, they will test their creativity.
- Are encouraged, their confidence will grow.
- Are praised for good work, they will improve their performance.
- Increase their performance, their self-esteem goes up.
- Receive fair treatment, their own decisions are more just.
- See supervisors who don't avoid accountability, they will be more responsible themselves.

Change Before You Must

"Every organization has to prepare for the abandonment of everything it does," says Peter Drucker.

That's tough. The longer we do something a certain way, the more difficult it is to change...the longer it takes us to change...and the more emotional we are about changing!

Faced with this resistance, leaders must work hard to set the tone for their organizations and coax them into new ideas, actions, and structures. Notice I said "coax," not "force."

Maybe the best recent example comes from the man credited with making famous the "Change before you have to" concept.

When Jack Welch took the reins as CEO at General Electric in 1980, he saw that the manufacturing era was coming to an end. Instead of relying on his company's clout to bully its way through, he faced up to the painful changes that would be demanded and made them faster and more emphatically than anyone else in business. Most people felt he was instituting change precipitously, but looking back, he wishes he had been even faster.

Welch made changes from top to bottom. He replaced GE's goal of being the world's biggest or fastest-growing company with a new one—becoming the world's most valuable company. He sold old businesses and entered new ones. He reworked GE's internal practices and culture in order to bring forth new ideas from individuals. To make GE competitive, he burned its five "blue books," which had guided GE managers since time immemorial. In their place, he inaugurated sessions that encouraged people to ask questions and make proposals on how to run the company better. GE employees learned that they had a right to speak up and be taken seriously.

Just after the turn of the century, this man who changed GE left so the organization could reinvent itself again. He said it should "repot itself, start again, get new ideas, renew itself. And I shouldn't stay on board." Once again, he wanted his company to change before it had to and he used his own life and career to prove his point.

When Is It Time to Change?

If you need to change before you must, then how do you know when that time comes?

Sometimes change comes out of frustration. A person may be tired of being overweight and out of shape. A company may be fed up with high expenses or low profits.

Sometimes an industry change forces a company to change. When Ben Roth of Roth Staffing found that customers were insisting on higher-quality temporary workers, he had to figure out how to change his industry...or just change with it. So he began to screen prospective temporary workers more carefully and pay them at or above market rate. Higher-performing staffers earn paid vacations and a 401(k) plan. To keep his corporate staff loyal and productive, he offered them equity in the business. And to manage offsite staffers, Roth set up offices on-site at his biggest clients, so placement could be handled conveniently.

Sometimes change is forced by a sale, merger or acquisition. T. Rowe Price focused on the future. In the early 1960's he gave attention to small company, "emerging growth" stocks in space exploration electronics and drugs. He liked innovation and invested in companies like Texas Instruments, Xerox and Hertz. His mutual funds took off like a rocket.

Sometimes change is the very air a company breathes. In his book, *Clock Speed*, MIT Professor Charles H. Fine introduced the term "industrial fruit flies" for businesses whose products may be outmoded within weeks or months of their launch and whose corporate lives seem continually at risk. In these companies, people change because they really have to.

Even if your organization isn't an industrial fruit fly, it may behoove you to act like one. When you get to the bottom line, **life is anticipation** and death is no change.

Time is not on your side. Change will come more quickly than you think. Whatever you think you want to do, get on with it! Abraham Lincoln said, "All things come to those who wait, but they get only what's left by those who hustle!"

Dennis Keller, the Chairman and CEO of DeVry, Inc remembers that since childhood he has always wanted to try new things. Early in his career, he was impressed by the practical, hands-on experience provided by the DeVry Institute of Technology owned by his employer, Bell and Howell. With prestigious degrees from Princeton and the University of Chicago, he saw a need to apply the DeVry approach to graduate business education. The Keller School of Management was established in 1973. It became the first for-profit educational institution ever admitted to the North Central Association of Colleges and Universities. In 1987, Keller and his partner, Ron Taylor, bought DeVry.

Keller was convinced that courses taught by practitioners (rather than full-time professors) for employed students would work. His judgment and confidence were right on. Keller and DeVry now form one of the largest publicly held higher education companies in the U.S.

Dennis complements his own enthusiasm by hiring high-energy 'internally driven' people. He wants them to question, challenge, and bring new ideas. He certainly has convinced me. Having done some teaching for him in the early '70's, I never thought he could pull it off. But he has…and then some!

Is It Time to Change?

- What is your organization doing that
  is no longer serving its purpose? Do
  you know? Do you have evidence?
  What is it?
- What is your work group doing that is
  not cost-effective or consistent with
  your organization's priorities?
- What are you doing personally that
  may be restricting your growth,
  limiting your future, and dulling your
  competitive edge?

Leaders Create Change

Leaders, not managers, create change.

A manager administers...a leader innovates.

A manager maintains...a leader develops programs.

A manager focuses on systems and structure...a leader focuses on people.

A manager relies on control...a leader inspires trust.

A manager has a short-range view...a leader has a long-range perspective.

A manager asks how and when...a leader asks what and why.

Former Senator Bill Bradley says, "Leadership means getting people to think, believe, see and do what they might not have without you."

According to Pulitzer Prize-winning historian James MacGregor Burns, there are two kinds of leaders—transactional and trans-formational. Transactional leaders have modest goals and enlist cooperation through deals like offering bonuses for reaching sales targets. They exemplify many of the qualities of managers just listed—administering, maintaining, controlling.

In contrast, transformational leaders "look for potential motives in followers, seek to satisfy higher needs, and engage the full person of the follower," says Burns. They don't put money or power as the first priority, although these may come their way. Instead, they are driven by the satisfaction of building an organization, seeing its people develop, and accomplishing things through others.

Magnet people conduct transactions when necessary, but other-wise are squarely in the transformational category. They value **results** *and* they keep their eyes on lofty, long-term goals. They have a clear vision of what they are trying to achieve and they do what it takes to transform people and organizations to achieve it.

Back in Chapter 1, I pointed out that a prime quality of magnet people is *trustworthiness*. This is an essential concept in assessing influence at any level.

Changing before you must takes trust. How else can a leader who sees the need to change before others do convince them to follow? The personal integrity and trust that are the capital of magnet people are drawn upon deeply in times of change. The greatest enemy of change is doubt. Its greatest asset is trust. Instigators of change must prove that they can be trusted—even though they may also be confronting a completely new challenge. For example, I am convinced that many of the people who stood by Bill Clinton's lies and deception in the depths of his presidency, did so for personal reasons, not loyalty. They knew he was terribly tarnished and wrong, but wanted to seem to be loyal in order to protect their political turf or career ambitions.

Alex Stonkus has learned a lot about how to motivate people to motivate themselves. Since joining Actrade in 1997 as Vice-President and Chief Operating Officer, sales have gone from $4 million to $32 million in three years and earnings from $.25 to $1.25 per share. To him the keys are:

1. Directly consulting the people who do the work; and
2. Holding people accountable for goals they help to set.

"It's amazing," he says, "what you can learn when you ask, "If you could, what would you do differently here?" His summary—"You've got to learn about the individuals and then be able to react to them."

Why Change Is Resisted

There are many reasons why change is resisted. Most have to do with the attitudes of people at the top.

Change is resisted when a leader:

- fails to show why a change is necessary
- fails to be specific about where we are now, where we need to be and how we can get there
- fails to allow those affected by change to have a say in the planning
- uses a personal appeal to gain acceptance of a change—for example, "Do me a favor and vote for my plan" or "Take my word for it; this will pay off big."
- fails to keep people informed about a change
- fails to allay worries about possible failure
- creates excessive work pressure during the change
- fails to deal with anxiety over job security.

Reducing Resistance to Change

There are ways to overcome or reduce resistance. Begin by recognizing that others may not share your beliefs or attitudes. Their beliefs and attitudes are habit patterns that may be difficult to alter. Discovering that old behavior is inadequate or new must be acquired will often trigger emotional tension and resistance.

Visualize the change from the viewpoint of those who will have to use or adapt to the new system or procedure. Take time to anticipate difficulties in getting acceptance and devise ways to make the transition more acceptable.

Carefully consider all the consequences. While there are exceptions to the rule, abrupt, sweeping change can be disruptive, even disastrous. It is almost always best to bring about changes gradually, one step at a time.

Talk with key people involved before you begin. Try to enlist their support first. Make sure you can clearly explain why a change is necessary, and provide a clear incentive to make it happen. When people understand why change is necessary—and exactly why they should do *what* they do and *how* it fits into the total picture—they are more likely to work together to help you accomplish it.

Maintain continuing contact with everyone affected by the change. They should know what will be different and why. People will accept new ideas and changes more easily if they are prepared for them. Avoid surprises.

Finally, pick your battles wisely. Change agents always meet resistance. The tough question to answer: Which forms of resistance deserve attention? Do I worry most about employee complaints? What if costs skyrocket? Will customers accept it? What if some of my best customers defect?

Here's an example. In response to low customer satisfaction and late orders, Doug Cahill, general manager of Olin Pool Products, invented a new organization "so flat you could stick it under a door," he says. First he explained to his top managers that he had collapsed 14 departments into eight process teams whose goal was to satisfy the customer, not the boss. In meeting with employees around the clock, they got a feeling that Cahill himself could be counted on.

Soon, both sales and profits increased dramatically. His managers believed him, so then he could count on them.

Angry people are always more vulnerable than those who are calm.

When Change Is Unexpected

Even magnet people sometimes have changes thrust upon them. A sudden illness. An unexpected personal loss. Even a job loss.

When sudden change strikes, don't panic. Resisting will likely get you nowhere. Instead of objecting to change, try to respond. Act with dignity and hold your head high.

Keep your eye on the future and seek to create it. Don't define yourself by what you can currently do and are doing. If you are only as good as your past, you deny the reality of change. As a high school dropout, my dad always believed he was doomed to work for a low hourly wage and take other peoples' orders and that's exactly what happened to him.

Change gives you an opportunity to redefine yourself. Create your own future, as big as you can dream it. Believe that you will get the resources to make it happen.

Finally, don't try to do it alone. Even the best leaders need help. Call in an experienced, objective coach with a good track record for support or tactical advice at critical times.

Use Everything You Have

In my years as a consultant, I've developed a list of what I consider to be the minimum essentials for personal development. Here they are:

1. A basic capacity to benefit from developmental contacts, exposures, and experiences
2. A strong sense of personal responsibility— willingness to work hard and devote "above average" amount of time and energy
3. A flexible or adaptive outlook conducive to using change itself as an element of growth
4. Time and opportunity to learn and grow.

All of these qualities are essential for personal development— because life calls upon us to use everything we have to meet its challenges and savor its pleasures. Test this statement. Do you know anyone who is truly successful in terms of results achieved who inherited their position without personal sacrifice? I don't.

Top athletes must draw on all their resources whenever they compete. Champion cyclist Lance Armstrong's mother used to tell him, "Make every negative a positive." According to Armstrong, "nothing goes to waste; you put it all to use; old wounds and long-ago slights become the stuff of competitive energy."

Likewise, five-time Olympic champion speed skater Bonnie Blair says, "My most important motivation comes from inside. I control my attitude. I bring everything I have to the starting line."

She brings everything she has to the starting line. Sadly, too many people don't even know how much they have to bring or have not started to develop it before they are "called to the starting line."

Our limits are largely self-imposed. We can change them by seeking out mentors whose wisdom and experience can help us set and achieve goals. One woman vice president I know felt her career was stalled "because" she was a woman. Her complaints changed nothing, but watching the most influential vice president in action did. When she used his ways, she got better results.

If you are not committed to getting better at what you are doing, you are bound to get worse.

—Pat Riley, Coach, Miami Heat

Study people you can learn the most from. Copy them. Surround yourself with high-quality people. Always be on the lookout for talented people, especially as members of your team. Your success as a leader is directly proportional to the success of your team. Build it. Prize it. It is absolutely critical to hire and nurture the very best you can find.

Keep an open mind and avoid falling into the trap of prejudice. Faced with change, too many organizations decide to pursue a solution before they understand the problem. Author Denis Waitley notes that this kind of prejudice—a judgment or opinion reached before the facts are known or maintained after the facts have changed—limits our ability to respond effectively to change. Waitley identified four "curses" of prejudice in *Personal Excellence* (April 1999):

1. Prejudice limits vision. It keeps us focused on what already exists or on something that we imagine exists, rather than on what might exist.
2. Prejudice stifles creativity. It insists that there is only one correct way of looking at problems when there are often many ways.

3. Prejudice prevents problem-spotting. Often leaders solve problems that aren't even clearly identified—they're simply "the way things are" and therefore the way people believe they have to be.
4. Prejudice restricts the flow of information. Prejudiced people choose to believe that they have all the relevant facts rather than open their minds to other ideas. People who've become prejudiced pay less and less real attention to the environment. They don't look for new patterns, notice inconsistencies, or ask why.

Go with what you have, but make sure you have something.

Stay optimistic. "Everything that has been accomplished in the world has been done by an optimist—nothing by a pessimist," said Goodyear Tire founder Franklin A. Seiberling in 1924. "It is easy to be pessimistic when things are breaking badly. Things can break badly for the optimist, but because of his optimism he can make them right themselves and come his way."

Finally, seek excellence. Ask the best from yourself. Accepting anything less than excellence means accepting mediocrity. Eleanor Josaitis founded Focus: Hope, a nonprofit program for the chronically underemployed who yearn for an opportunity to haul themselves into the middle class. Like a boot camp, her program expects students to meet demanding standards in academics, discipline, and responsibility. Profane language and theft are grounds for dismissal. Those who complete its job-training program find jobs.

Those who graduate from its highly regarded Machinist Training Institute find highly paid jobs in machining and metalworking in the auto industry.

Josaitis' program mixes compassion and discipline. It gives people a chance—while expecting standards to be met. It calls upon its students to use everything they have. So far, more than 6,000 people have responded. Very convincing proof!

Because I used "all I had" to recover from polio, I draw the most inspiration from stories of people with disabilities. Although she was born with spina bifida, Jean Driscoll learned to walk and even ride a bike. When a bicycle accident left her wheelchair bound at 15, she tried wheelchair basketball and hockey, and began competing in wheelchair racing. Strength training and a grueling 120-mile a week workout took her to victory in the 2000 Boston Marathon's women's wheelchair division. "I was born with a God-given, prove-me-wrong attitude—tell me I can't do that and I'm going to do it," she says.

Like most parents, Donna and Larry Posont spend lots of time caring for their five children. But because they are blind, they have had to invent some ingenious ways to handle day-to-day tasks like sorting laundry, shopping, playing catch, and making video recordings of soccer games and school plays. "No one is limited by blindness," says Donna. "We're only limited by attitude."

I say "amen." Approach life with the attitude that you will use everything you have and you will be amazed by how rich God has made you. My friends, Bob and Jennie Mahoney agree. They are both blind. They had ten children and are still living independently at 81 years of age!

Chapter 5

Magnet People Feel Secure

In the 1979 Cotton Bowl, quarterback Joe Montana sat shivering on the bench while his Notre Dame teammates struggled to overcome the University of Houston's 8-point lead. Prospects of a Notre Dame victory dimmed every minute that Montana, sick with the flu, sat on the sidelines.

Somehow, Montana summoned the strength to return to the game in the fourth quarter. In the last seconds of the game—and in one of the most amazing achievements in football—Montana threw a touchdown pass that was caught just as time expired on the clock.

What makes a person secure? In Joe Montana's case, it's more than desire. It's more than persistence. It's self-confidence, turned into action.

Circumstances provide the opportunity to test the depth and scope of security born of inner confidence. Too many people want proof that something will succeed before they try it. But most of the time there is no hard evidence. I've known magnet people who radiate confidence because they are so secure, so sure of their own abilities that they persist no matter what.

Confidence leads to optimism—another essential ingredient. "The final test of a leader is the feeling you have when you leave [their] presence after a conference," said Field General Bernard Montgomery. "Have you a feeling of uplift and confidence?" Montgomery knew what I have long suspected: cynicism and optimism are both contagious. Bonafide magnet people exude optimism, and they make sure the people around them are liberally "infected."

People like this make profound contributions to their enterprise, their family, their times—because their confidence and their character give them an authenticity that shallow people lack. To me, authentic people understand themselves and their values, can express themselves powerfully, and do not back off from challenges.

But some people let their self-confidence seal them off from useful feedback. Even the best quarterback needs support—and sometimes criticism—from the coach. That's why magnet people temper their self-confidence with the ability to listen for, and even encourage, constructive criticism.

A vital element of security is flexibility. Security is not rigidity. Quite the opposite. With security comes the possibility of change. Change doesn't threaten people who are secure. In the face of change, they—

- encourage constructive criticism
- don't punish risk takers
- create new options
- withhold rewards from change resistors.

It's interesting that most of these four qualities involve giving away power. You can't benefit from listening to others without accepting their credibility. You can't lift up risk takers or create new options unless you are ready for others to take a lead and run with it—perhaps in a different direction than you had in mind. And if you are going to withhold rewards from change resistors, then you must reward people who are flexible, adaptable…even though they may get in trouble from time to time as they lead you to new places you haven't imagined yet.

"No matter what kind of organization you run," says Robert Johnson founder and CEO of the Black Entertainment Television network, "you have to get others to buy into your vision and its potential, and infect them with the desire to succeed. You then have to balance being a taskmaster and a friend, and, at the right time, make them part of the decision-making and risk-taking process and let them share in the rewards."

In other words, you need to cut them in on the action. Insecure people keep others from significant participation. Secure people—magnet people—include them. They empower others and lead the way courageously into the future without fear of being overshadowed, or bypassed or undermined.

Power Pyramid... for Leaders

We

Thank you

Would you please

What would you suggest?

Encourage Constructive Criticism

The inability to listen has ruined many promising careers.

You may have confidence in your vision and be committed to it...but you aren't always right. Don't run scared from people who disagree with you. **There is no growth while you are protecting yourself from criticism or insulating yourself from mistakes.**

Magnet people can take criticism. They've mastered the ability to remain calm while receiving feedback. They stay open to what they hear. "If you're smart, you'll surround yourself with people who are caught up in the magic of your idea as much as you are," says Bob Lutz, former vice chairman of Chrysler. "But if you're *really* smart, you'll pick one person who's the one who says, 'Wait a minute, not so fast....' He or she can keep you from letting all that passion and excitement carry you off into trouble." In his years at General Motors, BMW, Ford, and Chrysler, Lutz saw plenty of great ideas stumble for lack of people willing to point out a flaw—and for lack of leaders willing to hear them.

Some naysayers should be dismissed, of course, but others may have bad news you need to hear. As a leader, you better get used to the heat. Acknowledge that you will be a prime target for criticism. No one is perfect. Everyone has flaws. If you stay open to criticism and can honestly recognize your weak points, you can delegate many of the tasks involving your weakness to people stronger in those areas.

If your goal is to avoid or suppress criticism, you are likely to feel discouraged, and angry, frustrated most of the time. Instead, encourage constructive criticism. Listen carefully. These guidelines will be helpful:

1. Take a deep breath and count until you calm yourself down.
2. Listen openly. You may not like it, but listen to it.
3. Don't take it personally. No matter how off-base you think the criticism is, resist the temptation to lash back. Former President Richard Nixon is a good example. He became so obsessed and angry with his critics that he focused on punishing them. His blindness to legitimate criticism ultimately caused him to make decisions that brought down his presidency.
4. Get a second opinion. Not everyone has your best interests in mind. Don't get defensive. Say, "Thanks for the feedback. I'll take some time to evaluate what you said and see if I should make any changes based on your suggestions." Then consult someone you trust to see what part, if any, of the criticism is valid.
5. Ask yourself, "What can I learn from this criticism?" Maybe a policy that turns off one customer also turns off others. When Gert and Tim Boyle were struggling to turn around the prospects of Columbia Sportswear after Neal Boyle's death, they listened to everyone—customers, bankers, even potential buyers of the company. Each time they learned how an

improvement could be made, they implemented it.
"Listening to others was the biggest part of the
turnaround," says Tim.

6. Take criticism in stride. Laugh and then delegate what
you can't do yourself to someone who may be able to
do it better.

Careful listening is especially important if you find yourself in a
position where you have less experience than those you are supposed
to lead. In these circumstances, asking questions is more effective
than inviting resentment by asserting authority. Admitting you don't
have all the answers will help build good relationships—which is a
key part of getting good results.

Invite people to talk. Ask how they think you're doing. When a
project ends, find out what they would like to have done differently.
With their input, come up with meaningful standards as a baseline
for tracking progress.

Listen. Listen. Listen. Soon you will be able to hold a meeting in
which you can summarize what has been said. Then you can present
a plan of action, based on their insights, summarizing where your
organization is now and where it needs to be in six months or a year.
This approach, coupled with clear standards for measurements, is a
key reason why magnet people are successful.

Not All Criticism Is Constructive

Some people prefer griping above all. No matter what the weather,
situation or occasion, they complain. It's their trademark.

Worse yet, their gripes command attention. Studies show that in
meetings, negative people are perceived as being smarter than positive
people—because being critical is so often interpreted as a sign of
intelligence. Especially in business, it seems that the fastest way for a
person to seem smart is to cut another one down. So person A comes
up with an idea, and person B comes up with a thousand different
reasons why that idea won't work. Soon everyone sees person A
as dumb and person B as smart—and no one wants to come up or
venture any new ideas for fear of being perceived as "stupid."

How can you encourage dissent and constructive criticism while discouraging chronic carping that leads nowhere? Constructive critics are made, not born. You can train and nurture them…if you're willing to show them. When it comes to constructive criticism, the lead mentor ought to be the boss. If an example of positive thinking is not set at the top, 1) critics and change resistors will prevail and 2) organizations become their own worst enemy.

Teach people how they can disagree without being disagreeable. The chief reason that "the enemy within" thrives and grows is because we have not learned how to be constructive critics. To show people, use the word *why* a lot, and ask for the evidence behind their claims.

Finally, don't shoot the messengers of bad news. If you do, the messenger is entitled to say, "Whoa, why are you picking on me? You said you wanted to hear the bad news. I gave you some and now you're punishing me."

When it's your turn to be the messenger, be straight. Don't hold back from saying something that is important just because you are worried about how you will express yourself or how your message will be received. Magnet people tell the truth and accept the truth when they hear it from others. Express yourself authentically—it will demonstrate a complete connection—what you say and what you do.

You can't learn from your mistakes if you refuse to admit you made any.

—Jason Zweig

Don't Punish Risk Takers

Change means risk, learning, and making mistakes.

Unfortunately, too many companies are unable to change because they keep their people on too short a leash. Make one mistake, and you're out.

This kind of punishment can be very subtle. Risk takers may be isolated. Made to feel they are not a team player. Or overlooked for promotion. Managers may say of a prospective candidate, "Wait a minute! Didn't she have that idea a couple of years ago that we could save $20,000 a year if we did such and such? Wasn't that her harebrained idea?" If this is reason enough to turn thumbs down, an organization might as well post a sign saying "No mistakes allowed." It's guaranteed to turn off the risk takers, the thinkers, and those who don't necessarily want tomorrow to be like today.

If you value change and innovation, you need to create a culture with a tolerance for error and failure. In order to come up with smart ideas and implement them quickly, people need permission to feel that all failures are not fatal.

Magnet people tolerate some mistakes. They tolerate inefficiency now and then and even occasional failure if it's creative and points in the right direction. They know that innovation always entails risk. When the prevailing motivation is safety and security you can bet that competitors are winning.

The answer: People need to be encouraged to try things they've never done before, things they may not do well the first time they try. In seeking an alternative to the transistor, Jack Kilby joined Texas Instruments in order to learn all he could about semiconductor materials like germanium and silicon. Long hours in the lab led him to experiment with silicon and eventually he was able to combine a transistor, capacitor and resistor onto a single silicon wafer in 1958. But an industry still reliant on transistors thought the new chips were expensive and unsuited to radios and televisions. Only more research and a new market—computers for the U.S. Air Force—enabled Kilby to perfect the chip until it cracked the consumer market in the first portable calculator in 1971.

In order to get people to try new things, you must banish fear. Studies clearly show that the greater their fear, the less likely people are to speak their mind or to create the kind of breakthrough concepts that win customers and grow profit margins. When people fear they will be punished for new ideas and actions, they simply won't try.

When fear is absent, change can be encouraged. Instead of promoting an environment of fear, seek to create an innovative climate where people feel safe enough to dream up and share ideas regularly. Robert Johnson, mentioned earlier, who created the Black Entertainment Television Network, urges people to create an environment where creativity is rewarded...where there are no bad ideas...where nothing is so outside the box that it's crazy, and where there can't be punishment, making someone feel isolated or not a team player. That philosophy has been so successful for Johnson that he is generally acknowledged to be the wealthiest African American.

Change is scary, but people will volunteer for dangerous tasks when they feel safe.

One way to stimulate creativity is to have experts listen to non-experts.

Throughout this book I've stressed the importance of results and accountability. While I remain a firm believer in both concepts, I know that **holding everybody accountable for their performance all the time may hamper innovation.** When it's time to learn new ways or try new approaches, back off a little. If you truly want people to learn, you'll have to remember that learning comes at a price. Learners are never as proficient as experts. Undoubtedly they will make mistakes. If people are going to be held accountable for every mistake they make, how many chances do you think they will take?

Another way to stimulate creativity and overcome fear is to have a contingency plan. If you go in with a plan for unexpected problems that may crop up, people can relax. Instead of fearing that you expect perfection—and freezing like a deer in the headlights when a mistake occurs—they can concentrate on trying new strategies, confident that the team is prepared to act if things start going wrong.

Three Thousand Years Without Risk—
A Story from the Internet

The U.S. standard railroad gauge is 4 feet 8.5 inches—a very odd number.

Why was that gauge used? Because that's the way they built them in England, and the U.S. railroads were built by English expatriates.

Why did the English people build them like that? Because the first rail lines were built by the same people who built the pre-railroad tramways, and that's the gauge they used.

Why did "they" use that gauge then? Because the people who built the tramways used the same jigs and tools that they used for building wagons, which used that wheel spacing.

Why did the wagons use that odd wheel spacing? Well, if they tried to use any other spacing the wagons would break on some of the old, long-distance roads, because that is the spacing of the old wheel ruts.

So who built those old rutted roads? The first long-distance roads in Europe were built by Imperial Rome for the benefit of their legions. The roads have been used ever since. And the ruts? The initial ruts, which everyone else had to match for fear of destroying their wagons, were first made by Roman war chariots. Since the chariots were made for or by Imperial Rome, they were all alike in the matter of wheel spacing.

Thus, we have the answer to the original question. The United States standard railroad gauge of 4 feet 8.5 inches derives from the original specs for an Imperial Roman army war chariot. Specs and bureaucracies live forever. So, the next time you are handed specifications and wonder what horse's ass came up with them, you may be exactly right. Because the Imperial Roman chariots were made to be just wide enough to accommodate the back ends of two war horses.

Create New Options

This story illustrates the main strategy used by people who don't want to make mistakes for fear of being punished: do things exactly the way they have always been done. This attitude creates many common responses to new ideas:

> *We've never done it that way.*
> *We're not ready for that yet.*
> *We're doing all right without it.*
> *We tried it once; it didn't work out.*
> *It costs too much.*
> *That's not (our/my) responsibility.*
> *Believe me, it won't work.*

Magnet people cut through these choruses. They see new possibilities and create new options. They find new ways to attack problems before a crisis occurs. They cut budgets and deadlines just to get people off autopilot and enable them to find new ways to do things. They shatter systems and find new paths in their quest to innovate.

They also involve many people intensely in that quest, because they know that in others lies a vast pool of new ideas waiting to be tapped. They know that the people who do the work are the best qualified to improve it. And that people who have opportunities within the organization are the ones who will develop themselves to the fullest potential...remain committed to their goals and objectives...and savor a higher level of job satisfaction.

Really great people make you feel

that you, too, can become great.

—Mark Twain

The primary tool of development for magnet people is decentralization—giving people the responsibility to make decisions on their own. In the end, all development is self-development. There's no way someone can experience another person's growth.

To magnet people, the talents of others are the backbone of an organization. As the New York Times says of Bill Gates, "Microsoft's only factory asset is the human imagination." Peter Drucker made the same point when he noted that unlike factory workers, knowledge workers—like the people who work for Microsoft—"*own* the means of production. It is the knowledge between their ears. It is totally portable and an enormous capital asset."

Tom Peters claims that the greatest breakthrough products are invented for the sheer joy of creating. When they co-founded Apple in 1976, inventors Steven Jobs and Steve Wozniak were playing around making toys for themselves and others like them. Their toy turned out to be a business tool that changed the world.

Creating new options can be fun. Seattle's Pike Place Fish Market is renowned for an environment that fosters employee loyalty and customer satisfaction. Instead of keeping employees and customers on separate sides of the counter, the Fish Market calls upon both parties to be co-creators of their shopping experience.

Instead of sticking to the well-known limits of employee behavior, sales or products, companies like Pike Place Fish Market seek new methods. When sales slowed and a temporary layoff seemed imminent, employees volunteered to get on the phones and drum up sales.

To develop your organization, give others a chance to spread their wings.

John Bogle, founder of the Vanguard Group, loves to ask customers for their ideas. Alfred P. West, Jr., founder of SEI Investments, flattened his company's management structure in order to institute a new culture he called "Let's try it." To promote new leaders, he created self-managed teams that let people figure out their strengths and use them. This 'fluid leadership' approach allows a number of leaders to come forward during a project, each one at the moment when his or her strengths are needed.

James Morgan, CEO of Applied Materials Inc., believes helping people in his organization meet their potential is his primary motivation. He takes the job seriously. To keep everyone thinking, he asks employees to spend five percent of their day "envisioning the future." People are expected to have three things they are thinking about but are not yet taking action on. To improve the quality of Applied Materials' products, he gave engineers a share in the success of the product.

There is no substitute for human creativity, adaptability, imagination and resourcefulness.

Magnet people believe that people who are callously stuffed into roles and job descriptions and treated as replaceable will focus on self-protection instead of on possibilities.

Never risk, never gain!

Confidence Grows with Achievement
We grow as we complete increasingly complicated tasks.

That's why, in a climate of change, people willing to innovate need continuing support. People who drag their feet, who resist change, who actively throw up barriers to impede innovation...should *not* be supported.

When Alfred P. West realized that the company he founded in 1966 was suffering from "a hardening of the arteries" and not adapting well to its changing environment, he took dramatic steps to reinvent and reinvigorate SEI Investments. During the restructuring, the company was torn apart and rebuilt with a new entrepreneurial spirit—and West's leadership was severely tested. He knew where he wanted to go, and he was willing to part ways with those who disagreed. During the three-year transition, nearly half of its employees left.

"Those were the people who did not want change," West says. Besides examining every aspect of the company's business and its prospects, West moved his company into new headquarters that had no walls, rubber floors, and furniture on wheels so it could be moved as needed. There are no floor plans, permanent seating charts or secretaries. People use a software program to track each other's whereabouts.

It sounds draconian, but it's working. "If you're totally comfortable, then somebody's going to sneak up behind you," says

West. "If you're not innovating, that means you're going to be left behind.

Many employees understandably resist a top-to-bottom transformation like this one. They don't know what the future holds, or where they fit into the new scheme. But even smaller changes meet some resistance. The key to implementing change successfully is to pick your battles wisely. Not every form of resistance deserves your attention. "If the brightness on your screen is always at full intensity, you can't tell what is highlighted," says Patricia Sueltz of IBM. In other words, modify your reaction as circumstances indicate. If it's a serious resistance that threatens all your plans, take on the challenge. But if you're hearing minor griping that will fade away with time, save your energy.

Instead of cutting them off, remain confident in those who are ambivalent about change. Or match them with an advisor/mentor who is comfortable with change. Let mild resisters know you believe they can meet your high standards and thrive during change. Tell them, "This is a tough job and I know you can do it."

People tend to rise or fall to their level of expectation.

Reward mediocrity and that's what you will continue to get.

Achievers expect a lot of themselves. Failures typically don't set goals so they won't be disappointed. Likewise, the best managers do not reward mediocrity. They may tolerate it temporarily, but they differentiate sharply in favor of those who get the best results.

Create an environment where they can bask in the glow of their own success. Do, and you'll find that a lot of people will step up and try things they probably never would have attempted before.

Pediatric physician Larry Wolk had a vision of providing health care in poorer areas at minimal costs to patients. To achieve his vision, he launched the nonprofit Rocky Mountain Youth Medical & Nursing Consultants, which serves 30,000 kids a year at school-based clinics and homeless shelters in a 40-foot long mobile unit that travels throughout rural Colorado.

Along the way to his dream, he learned several lessons about setting and reaching goals. First, if you have a dream, pursue it. You can realize it if you have a strong desire and the determination to make it real.

Next, turn a deaf ear to naysayers. "A goal or challenge is like a puzzle," Wolk says. "When you first look at it, you think it can't be done. I feel there's always a solution. No matter what the situation is, there's a way it can be worked out. It might not always be pretty, but it can get done."

Finally, find and work with people who think the way you do. Together, you can help one another through dark pessimistic times…and share each other's energy as your achievements nurture your confidence.

There is only one source of security. It lies within you. Sometimes it sleeps. Confidence wakes it up. Achievement keeps it growing.

It's not easy...

- to apologize
- to begin over
- to admit error
- to keep trying
- to take advice
- to be unselfish
- to be charitable
- to face a sneer
- to forgive mistakes
- to be considerate
- to endure success
- to profit by mistakes
- to keep out of a rut
- to forgive and forget
- to think and then act
- to make the best of little
- to subdue an unruly temper
- to recognize the silver lining
- to shoulder a deserved blame

It's not easy—but it is the way we grow.

How to Beat the Odds:

- Become a bullet biter
- Select friends carefully
- Be careful who you learn from
- Listen to those who love you
- Know before you talk
- Don't experiment with values
- Don't curse adversity
- Never substitute excuses for hard work
- Learn where to find what you don't know
- THINK
- Never compromise morals
- Respect only those who earn it
- Make persistence your legacy
- Don't delay—perform

Chapter 6

It's Your Move

A free society must have leaders at all levels who exemplify the five qualities featured in this book. Genuineness—Diligence—Objectivity—Unselfishness and Security.

But how do we ensure a continuing source for these people? Answer...we incubate them by first identifying role models of magnetic behavior and copying it. For example:

Magnet people find ways to renew themselves steadily and continuously

What to look for:

- They are not resistant to praise but don't require it.
- They appreciate flattery but don't seek it.
- They find new ways to attack problems before a crisis occurs.
- They accept credit when it is due but share it with those who helped them.
- They believe humility should increase with talent.

Magnet people are not ambiguous

What to look for:

- They want to be clear, to be understood.
- They do not "spin" circumstance in their favor.
- They do not discredit facts.
- They do not believe that the meaning of the 10 Commandments is relative.
- They defend what is right vs. "political correctness."
- They show appreciation more by action than words.

Magnet people are enablers

They have an overriding and prevailing conviction that helping others who are willing to help themselves is the best route to progress. What to look for:

- They ride to success on the shoulders of those they have helped.
- They are successful because they use the advice they give others.
- They bring others to the mountaintop with them.
- They are as easy to follow in bad times as in good times.
- They do supportive things that count, but don't stop to count them.
- They support problem solvers, not problem bringers.

Magnet people are committed to sustained goodness

They are as careful about granting privileges as they are withholding them. What to look for:

- They are accessible for counsel, but remote from petty arguments.
- They do not abuse power.
- They do not try to make themselves great by showing how small someone else is.
- They inspire self-confidence (not dependence) from those who follow them.
- They can say "no" and retain respect.
- They divert attention from themselves to those who do the work.

Magnet people are humbled by knowledge
What to look for:
- They appreciate what they already have.
- They believe the first qualification for leaders is self-control.
- They do not need constant admiration.
- They understand that self-control is most difficult in times of success.
- They can sometimes convert adversaries into supporters.

Magnet people are prepared for success
What to look for:
- They are willing to be measured by the amount of opposition they can withstand.
- They are comfortable being judged by what they finish, not what they attempt.
- They do not believe that success is a matter of luck.
- They believe tomorrow's choices are shaped today.
- They do what they say they will do.
- They never take a single defeat as final.

If I had but two wishes for you, I would wish: 1) that this book will make you more successful in finding and associating with people who have magnet qualities; and 2) that you will become one yourself. May they both come true!

About the Author

Roger Fritz is considered one of the country's foremost authorities on Performance Based Management and change requirements for individuals. Organizations from Fortune 500 companies to family-owned businesses have used his advice. Dr. Fritz has served over 300 clients and takes time each month for keynote, workshop and seminar presentations. His features in monthly magazines and weekly columns in business newspapers reach millions of readers. His 35 published books, translated into 17 languages, include several best sellers, book-of-the-month selections and award winners.

Roger passionately believes that *life is anticipation* and reveals in many captivating ways how that powerful principle changes lives and prompts success. His presentations feature unique combinations of humor, inspiration, practical advice and the impact of personal accountability.

He is founder (1972) and president of Organization Development Consultants 1240 Iroquois Drive, Suite 406, Naperville, IL 60563 • Phone: 630-420-7673 • Fax: 630-420-7835 • E-mail: RFritz3800@aol.com • Website: http://www.rogerfritz.com

Index

Nelson, Willie 21
Nightingale, Florence 63

objectivity 111
opposition 113
optimism 24, 93
optimist 91
options 102
Orfalea, Paul 62
Organization Civility Index (OCI) 49
originality 4

Papada III, James 15
Pearson, Christine 48
Peary, Adm. Robert E. 3, 28
performance 34, 54, 60
persistence 21, 93
pessimist 91
Peters, Tom 103
political correctness 111
Posont, Donna and Larry 92
Powell, Gen. Colin 11
power 11, 23, 25, 94-95, 112
praise 71
prejudice 90-91
Price, T. Rowe 80
problems 48, 52

recognition 70
Register, John 37
regrets 24
rejection 28

Additional Information

For more information about Dr. Roger Fritz's consulting and presentation topics or for a catalog of books, audio tapes, CD-ROMS, reprints, software and other products, contact:

Organization Development Consultants

Phone: 630.420.7673

Fax: 630.420.7835

Email: RFritz3800@aol.com

Website: http://www.rogerfritz.com
